How to Shoot
a Movie
and Video Story

Bill Duss
Randall 3.7 A
'87

The authors thank:

The late Ernie Pittaro, cameraman, and Morgan & Morgan editor, for his invaluable assistance in preparing the text and illustrations for this book,

and Dean Gaskill, news, documentary, and commercial cameraman, for his expert counsel on the video state of the art.

How to Shoot a Movie and Video Story

The Technique of Pictorial Continuity

By Arthur L. Gaskill
and David A. Englander

Photographs & Drawings by
Irving Levine

Additional Pictures by
David A. Marlin
and
Dean Gaskill

MORGAN & MORGAN, INC., Publishers
Dobbs Ferry, New York

First Edition 1947
Second Edition 1959
Third Edition 1960
Fourth Edition 1985

Library of Congress Cataloging in Publication Data

Gaskill, Arthur L., 1909 –
How to shoot a movie and video story.

1. Cinematography. I. Englander, David A.
II. Title.
TR850.G367 1984 778.5'23 84-27365
ISBN 0-87100-239-6

Morgan & Morgan, Inc., Publishers
145 Palisade Street
Dobbs Ferry, New York 10522

Type set and printed by
Morgan Press, 145 Palisade Street, Dobbs Ferry, N.Y. U.S.A.

CONTENTS

INTRODUCTION: A MUST
FOR THE READER

When the original HOW TO SHOOT A MOVIE STORY first appeared in 1947, there was no such thing as commercial television. The word "video" was unknown to the public. The book was written for home film makers, primarily the veterans and civilian war workers of World War II.

These were the millions of men and women who, with victory, had returned happily to the pleasures of home and family. They wanted the fun and excitement of telling a *movie* story about their loved ones as well as making a pictorial record with still photos. Fortunately, there was a variety of excellent, easy-to-use moderately priced camera equipment on the market, some of it meant specifically for home use like the 8mm camera.

The message of HOW TO SHOOT A MOVIE STORY to these aspiring cameramen and camerawomen was simple and basic: that there is far more to shooting a movie story than the mechanics of camera operation, like knowing how to set correct focus and exposure. To tell a movie story, you had to use the technique of pictorial continuity. With it, you could achieve a smooth, meaningful flow that give your story a professional look; without it, your film would appear awkward and amateurish no matter how expensive or elaborate your equipment was.

The message took hold. The book found a home not only with the postwar generation but with their children, the new generation of the famous "baby boom." They became film buffs, eager to learn the professional aspects of film making, perhaps, with a desire to make it a career.

While these baby boom kids grew up in the '50s and '60s, the great new visual medium of television was maturing at the same time. Some members of this generation went to work in television operating the ponderous studio cameras of the time or directing the cameras. They learned—just as their film maker peers did—that whether you were shooting scenes live or on videotape (or film for broadcast use), without pictorial continuity you could not achieve that smooth visual flow so agreeable to the eye.

The same learning experience was waiting for the home video cameraman when compact, lightweight, portable (and affordable) video cameras came into their own in the '80s, attaining a popularity rivalling film cameras.

The plain fact is that pictorial continuity is a "must" technique any time you tell a story by means of a series of moving images projected on a viewing surface normally rectangular in shape. It doesn't matter whether the viewing surface is a giant screen in a theater or of the modest dimensions of a home TV set. Nor does it matter that the process of creating those moving images is chemical in the case of film and electronic in videotape. Both ways, you have a *motion picture*, and the rules of pictorial continuity apply equally. To make that perfectly clear, the original text was revised and its title changed to HOW TO SHOOT A MOVIE AND VIDEO STORY.

You'll notice that the word "movie" in the title is given its old-time meaning of a story shot on film. That's because the meaning of long familiar words changes slowly. People, including professionals, still think of a movie in its traditional, pre-video sense. When they refer to video, they try to differentiate between the two media by saying that film produces "motion pictures" and videotape gives us "moving images." With respect, we've got to say that's kind of silly—and futile. Both expressions reduce to the simple word "movie" and we believe it is inevitable that a movie will come to mean a story shot on either film or videotape.

The trend in that direction is already under way and, at the risk of offending some word purists, we're going to give that trend a friendly nudge in this book. Anytime you see the word *movie* or *motion picture,* it implies both film and video. Whenever we want to make a distinction between the two media, we'll be specific about it, using the terms film or video (also videotape).

Regarding another aspect of word usage, please note that solely for expediency's sake words like *his* or *cameraman* may appear herein that refer to both sexes. We do not wish to offend our female readers and we hope they will understand.

Anyway, the issue here is not semantic subtleties but the commonality of both film and video in requiring pictorial continuity. We'll put it in a sweeping statement: pictorial continuity is the indispensable framework of every soundly constructed motion picture, whether it is a Hollywood feature, a made-for-TV-movie, a TV news story, a documentary, a cartoon or, of course, a home movie.

That is indeed a big statement but don't let it worry you if you're a beginner or student. Pictorial continuity is easy to learn and easy to use. It does demand some time, patience and thought, but it's a piece of cake compared to absorbing technical stuff about camera optics or electronics, the chemistry of film, the electromagnetic properties of videotape and so forth.

Shooting a movie or video story is a creative process. It should be fun and excitement once you've mastered its technique. Besides, you'll have the most gratifying reward a cameraman can receive: your audience will enjoy watching your story!

CHAPTER 1

PICTORIAL CONTINUITY: THE SIMPLE SEQUENCE

THE MEANING OF CONTINUITY

Most people who have pressed the button of either a still or movie camera appreciate the fact that a motion picture is only a series of still pictures in which the change between the frames is so slight that the illusion of motion is gained. Videotape does not have images or frame lines visible to the unaided eye, but when played back it produces the same optical illusion of motion.

However a good motion picture is more than just a series of animated snapshots. It hangs together, it tells a story smoothly, coherently, logically. The know-how of this is contained in the technique of *pictorial continuity.*

Pictorial continuity is a rather fancy term, but we like it, because it states so precisely what we're out to describe. The dictionary explains "continuity" as an "uninterrupted, close union of separate parts." Pictorial continuity, therefore, in a fully rounded definition, would be *the proper development and connection of motion-picture sequences to create a smoothly joined, coherent motion-picture story.*

BASIC ELEMENTS OF THE SIMPLE SEQUENCE

Mr. Producer

| *The Long Shot* | *The Medium Shot* | *The Close-up* |

BASIC ELEMENTS OF THE SEQUENCE

Defining more closely, we use the dictionary description of a "sequence" as a "series of things following in a certain order or succession," and we therefore term our motion-picture sequence a *related series of shots*. The sequence thus is a fundamental unit in pictorial continuity. And it has three simple basic elements: the long shot, the medium shot, and the closeup. We break down the sequence this way because all people view action in real life with their eyes in terms of long shot, medium shot, and close-up, even if they do not realize it.

Grasp these elements, and their correct logical use, and you have caught the basic idea. They are elementary, but you cannot start without learning them. They are the ABC's of continuity; the XYZ's will come in due time.

THE LONG SHOT

We say these elements are simple and that they correspond to the stages by which the human eye views action. Let's prove it by shooting a simple sequence.

We will use two admirable photographic instruments. First, we'll shoot with the greatest, most inimitable camera of them all—the human eye. Then we'll shoot the same action with either a film or video camera.

Now for our action. We want something ordinary and everyday, such as visiting an office. You are calling to apply for a job, to give a sales pitch, or perhaps to persuade a movie producer to back a movie you want to make!

You enter the door of Mr. Producer's office. The scene is new to you, so you hesitate for an instant to orient yourself and satisfy your curiosity. *Your eye has automatically started to shoot.* In a split-second glance, it has taken in the room, registering walls, windows, desk, and most important, the man behind the desk. In short, your eye has established the locale[1] or setting and your subject in it.

Now your camera must do for a movie audience what your eye did for you. It must provide an *establishing shot*[2] so that your audience will see on screen what your eye saw in real life and recognize the scene instantly as an office.

The establishing shot is usually a *long shot,* an "LS."

Okay, let's get started. Pick up your camera and guided by what you see in the viewfinder, shoot an LS of the office.

Don't move your camera too fast! Shoot what your eye sees, but don't try to shoot it *in the same way*. There's no camera in existence that can imitate your eye in throwing a glance around the room with lighting speed. Try it with your camera and you'll have a weird, waving effect (blurred, too, if you do it fast enough) that will force your audience to shut its eyes because it is so painful to look at.

Many an over-ambitious but under-experienced beginner has lost his audience by selling his cameraman's soul for a flashy "pan" when it was uncalled for. (See explanation of panning in Chapter 8). You'll find justification for the pan further along in the book, but not on this occasion.

Right now, your LS can be taken from a nice, steady, stationary position.[3] From where you stand in the doorway, you are far enough back to take in your subject and a great deal of his surroundings—enough to establish the locale.

If you are fussy about composition, you can move back even more, and shoot the office interior with the doorway as a frame on either side. It won't be worth it, though, if you cut off too much of the interior, or if your subject is so far away that he seems lost. It is, after all, *his* office, he dominates *it*. You don't want to suggest the reverse. This is just a simple story, not a deep, dark psychological drama.

By now, the long shot and its function should be well established in your mind. Go on into the office, with your eye again doing the shooting.

You and your eye want to get as close to your subject as you can. As you move in toward Mr. Producer, your eye instantly, automatically, and continuously keeps readjusting itself to the changing perspective and proportions of the scene. It takes in increasingly more and more of Mr. Producer, his face, hair, shoulders, tie, shirt, the articles on his desk, and less and less of the rest of his surroundings, such as the wall, the window, and the bulk of the desk.

This in the way you want it. After all, the vital part of the scene is Mr. Producer, not his location. You want to cut out as much of the extraneous, distracting locale as you can, and come as close to his face as your eye, and politeness, will allow. This is your closeup, the heart of your picture.

THE MEDIUM SHOT

But before discussing the closeup, we must look at the technique by which we duplicate the eye's transition from long shot to closeup with the camera. This brings up the inevitable question. Why is a transition shot needed at all?

The argument is as follows: We say that the closeup is the heart of the picture. We take the LS, which no one disputes is essential for establishing the location of the scene. So, once the scene is established, why waste the audience's time and the cameraman's film or videotape on a transition shot? Why not go *directly* to the closeup?

It is a good question, but one which overlooks a vital factor. Never forget that your camera is mimicking the human eye. Suppose you were suddenly blindfolded as you stood at the door of Mr. Producer's office; then his charming secretary took you by the hand, led you right up to him, and abruptly removed the blindfold so that you found yourself staring at Mr. Producer within a foot of his face. What would your reaction be?

You would certainly be lost momentarily. The jump from the general long shot to the intimate, concentrated closeup would have been too much for the eye. Instinctively, it would seek to reorient itself by backing up in order to place Mr. Producer in relation to his surroundings.

Now suppose an audience, looking at your movie on the screen is suddenly confronted with that closeup after seeing the long shot. It cannot reorient itself outside the boundaries of the screen. Imagine how much greater the shock would be for it!

No, this great jump will not do. It is too abrupt. There must be a midway or transition shot—the *medium shot.*

What do you do then—mimic the eye as it moves from long shot to closeup by grinding away constantly with your camera as you move in on Mr. Producer? That would be wasteful, tedious, and give a very jumpy picture, unless you used a special device such as a "dolly" or a zoom lens. The "dolly" is a stable platform on wheels which keeps your camera steady as it moves. The zoom lens enables you to move in close on the subject without moving your camera.[4] You probably have a zoom lens on your camera. Please don't use it here! The human eye is not a zoom lens (except for Superman). To get a closer look at Mr. Producer you have to move toward him. Do the same with your camera. Carry it about halfway toward him and shoot your MS from there.

By moving closer to your subject, you eliminate a lot of background detail no longer of interest. What is more, your subject grows larger on the screen; interest is being concentrated on him; and smoothly, naturally, unobtrusively, he is being built up for the ultimate closeup.

The medium shot, or "MS," is *a transition shot bridging the jump from long shot to closeup, and building up the subject.*

Before proceeding, it is essential to clear up any uncertainty about just where to place the MS. The medium shot, like so many other terms in motion pictures, is elastic in meaning. It does not have to be a mathematical half of the distance between long shot and closeup; it can be nearer either one, whichever serves the purpose better. It depends on the circumstances; long shot, medium shot, and closeup are all relative. Bear in mind only that you want your transition to be smooth, and your subject to be built up gradually.

For the case in point, an MS taking in the top of Mr. Producer's desk and a little of the background suits your purpose nicely. The desk is now not just another piece of furniture, but the main prop to set off—and focus attention on—Mr. Producer.

THE CLOSEUP

It is the *closeup,* the "CU," to which the LS and MS, properly executed, pave the way.

Your eye, we noted, came as close to Mr. Producer as it could. And that closeness created intimacy and warmth. Your eye's CU gratified a natural urge to see him from a point where his facial expressions might be studied closely and in detail.

Thus when the camera takes its closeup, your audience will see Mr. Producer's face, his head and shoulders filling the screen, his every expression vivid and alive. In the full meaning of the term, he will be "big as life." Certain things about his appearance that might have been vague or lost to the audience in a long or medium shot, will now strike the audience with great emphasis and clarity. It, too, will be face to face with Mr. Producer and be able to observe and respond to the play of emotion his face shows. The closeup is the most revealing, most expressive of motion-picture shots.

This seems so obvious today that it may be surprising to learn that the closeup was unknown in the early years of movie making until David W. Griffith introduced it, thereby revolutionizing the art. So don't take it for granted. Some beginning cameramen, especially those interested only in shooting family movies, tend to neglect the CU in favor of the LS and MS in order to "keep everyone in the picture."

This is not a hint to go to the opposite extreme. Because it is so powerful, the CU should be used discriminately, not frittered away through overuse. Too many CUs create visual monotony and slow down the flow of a motion picture story. An unrelieved succession of CUs is too much like a series of still picture snapshots. In addition, an excess of CUs at the expense of establishing shots can confuse your audience as to time and place; viewers become disoriented.

The danger of disorientation is present in a simple movie of baby at play, just as much as it is in an action feature shot on many different locations. You may say that it's only a home movie; why waste film or tape on long and medium shots to establish rooms familiar to you through a thousand comings and goings? The baby is the story, so why not get to those closeups right away?

But the friends and relatives you invite in for a screening aren't that familiar with your home. If someone has to ask where a particular scene was taken, then you have weakened audience interest in your story; you have goofed as a cameraman.[5]

NOT BY THE NUMBERS

Granted, you may say, that the basic elements of the sequence are simple, fundamental, and necessary; nevertheless isn't this one-two-three routine of LS, MS and CU too rigid, stiff, too much "by the numbers?"

It's a pertinent question. But that one-two-three pattern isn't inflexible. There can be lots of leeway in applying it, lots of room for imagination. We already pointed out that the medium shot is elastic in meaning. (A shot be-

tween an MS and a CU, but closer to the CU, is simply termed a *close shot.*[6])
Similarly, although we earlier cited the long shot as being used to establish a
scene, an establishing shot need not always be a long shot; there are times
when a medium shot will do as well or even be more suitable. The last thing in
the world we want you to do is to shoot as a matter of mechanical routine, according to rigid measurements! But you did have to learn to crawl before you
walked, and you've got to learn your long shot, medium shot and closeup procedure before going on to more complex phases of continuity.

Thus, as you read on, you will discover how to get all the flexibility you
want into the simple sequence, through what you will learn about the varied
technique of shooting and, ultimately, through what you will find out about
editing, that final assembling of your shots in the length and order that you
desire.

AUDIENCE REACTION
AND ACCEPTANCE

It cannot be reiterated too often that the camera-
man must enable his audience to see his work not only as he sees it thru his
viewfinder, but as he sees it *in his mind's eye.* Don't count on ESP in your audience; it can't read your mind. It can follow the story you're trying to tell only
from what it sees; it is completely dependent on the screen for understanding.

This fact is a great advantage to the moviemaker. He can control the reaction of his audience by what his footage depicts and by the way he arranges his
shots when he changes his role of cameraman to that of editor.[7] However, he
will throw away this power of audience control unless he keeps it informed *pictorially.* In other words, the action his audience sees onscreen should be *self-
explanatory.*

This holds true whether you're shooting a simple home movie for family or
friends, a more polished job for a local camera club, or an ambitious production aimed at commercial release.

Don't depend on a sound track of dialogue or narration (or yourself as an
off-screen voice if you haven't sound equipment) to do the job for you.

To be sure, many movie stories require dialogue for development of plot
or character; or in the case of documentaries, voiceover narration to convey information to the audience. But dialogue and narration are accessories to the
visual image; they should be used sparingly. The more the visual image tells
your story, the more interesting the story will be to its viewers.

All this emphasis on audience reaction and understanding may seem irrelevant to a cameraman who isn't interested in showing his work to an
audience. . . . We haven't met one yet!

The best way to understand the audience point of view is to edit the
footage you shoot. As your own editor, you will be the first audience to look at

your work. You can see your mistakes, your lapses in continuity, the shots you missed or did poorly and take corrective action. That is one of the marvels of videotape. You can see your footage immediately after you shoot it.

ACTION—NOT POSING!

There is a word we have used with great familiarity, a word describing something so inherent in motion-picture continuity, so much taken for granted, that it is often passed by without proper mention. The word is *action.* Let us hold onto it for a moment and give it due emphasis.

It is a characteristic of the animated-snapshot, pseudo-movie to have the subjects *posing,* doing nothing but standing or sitting stiffly—or even worse—staring into the camera.

(The very bad thing about staring into the camera is that the audence immediately perceives that the actor is *aware* of the camera. This destroys that enjoyable illusion of being privileged to peep into a scene wherein the players are unconscious of spectators; it destroys the scene's naturalness.)

The solution is simple. Have your subject *do something* that comes naturally. It doesn't have to be a "big" action; anything suitable to the story and which fits into the action will do. Have Mr. Producer write a note, check a manuscript or use the phone. Even though he may sit motionless as he listens to the phone, his attitude suggests action.

Giving your subject a natural action to perform relaxes him, diverts his attention from the camera and makes the scene appear to be completely lifelike.

ABOUT THE ORGANIZATION OF THIS BOOK

We have been arbitrary in deciding on the order in which we will discuss the various phases of pictorial continuity, and we have had to be. For one authority will argue that study of the general rule should precede overlap, the next will state the reverse, and a third will firmly declare that understanding of cut-ins and cut-aways should come before either. It is impossible to agree on the relative importance of these various subjects. All aspects of pictorial continuity are so closely interrelated that we must study the subject in its entirety. For our purpose we have placed the chapters in an order of precedence which, we are certain, presents the study of pictorial continuity in a logical manner and will, at the end of this book, enable you to see it as a whole.

VIDEO AS WELL AS FILM

Even though we're just warming up to the subject in this first chapter, it should be obvious to the video cameraman as well as the film cameraman that pictorial continuity is a must for both if he wants to tell a movie story.

If you've read the introduction, we're repeating ourselves. If you haven't (yes, we too sometimes skip introductions because they seem to delay getting into the book), *please go back and read it!* It brings into sharp focus why video and film cameramen are brothers under the skin even though their cameras are so different technically.

But there's no reason the video cameraman can't be comfortable shooting with the film cameraman's equipment and vice versa. All that's needed is guidance in the operating characteristics of each type of camera and some familiarization drill.

SUMMARY

In order for a film or video movie to be more than just a series of animated snapshots, it must have pictorial continuity.

• Pictorial continuity is the proper development and connection of motion-picture sequences to create a smoothly flowing, coherent motion-picture story.

• The sequence is a fundamental unit of continuity and has three basic, all-important elements: long shot, medium shot, and closeup.

• An establishing shot shows the audience the locale of the action and is usually a long shot.

• The cameraman must never forget that he must enable the audience to see action on the screen the same way he saw it while shooting. The movie should tell the story; action should be self-explanatory.

• To avoid the "animated snapshot" type of movie, the cameraman should have his subjects *do* something, instead of posing in stilted fashion. He must aim for action. And by giving the subject a natural action to perform, the scene will be much more lifelike.

• The reader will find that the apparent routine of the LS, MS, and CU is not inflexible. Pictorial continuity allows plenty of leeway, a theme that will be developed in succeeding chapters.

• Despite the technical differences in their equipment, film and video cameramen have a common bond—the use of pictorial continuity to tell a movie story.

CHAPTER 2

THE SIMPLE SEQUENCE: VARIATIONS

RELATIVITY

Having looked at the sequence in its simplest, most rudimentary form, we turn now to the problem of adding variety and interest. The long shot, the medium shot, and the closeup are all *relative,* as we've indicated. Translated, this means that the distances which separate the long shot from the medium and the medium shot from the closeup in an interior sequence such as visiting Mr. Producer would be different from the distances involved outdoors in photographing a parade where the LS from the rooftop might be hundreds of feet distant, the MS of the marching ranks from the sidewalks might be fifty feet away, and the final CU as much as twenty feet removed.

Long distances between shots do not necessarily typify outdoor sequences. The distances involved in shooting a parade do not apply in shooting an outdoor sequence of the neighbors' kids playing hopscotch on the sidewalk.

Nor are all indoor sequences restricted in distances between shots. The LS, MS, and CU are vastly different between filming a graduation exercise in a school auditorium and doing a sequence of a youngster assembling a toy rocket in the family playroom.

An indoor sequence like the graduation exercise, moreover, would call for greater distances between shots than an outdoor sequence showing the youngster testing his rocket in the back yard.

Relativity applies as truly to the simple, solid facts of moviemaking just as it does to the abstruse world of mathematical physics. The point to remember is that relativity depends strictly on the personal preference of the cameraman and what he wants to emphasize in his movie.

Take the case of Roscoe and Ross, two young cameramen who set out to shoot the same sequence about Roscoe's newly purchased sports car. Roscoe's sister Pam is in the scene, both for eye appeal and to provide human interest.

Proud owner Roscoe intends to shoot his car as a TV commercial, hoping to sell it to the dealer. Conscious of the photogenic background that sets off

RELATIVITY
Two Treatments of the Same Story

Below—Ross's Sequence
  Long Shot
  Medium Shot
  Closeup

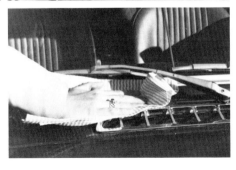

Above—Roscoe's Sequence
  Long Shot
  Medium Shot
  Closeup

the car, he shoots his LS far enough back to take in the house as well as trees and shrubs. Then he moves into an MS in which the car, with its sporty lines, dominates the scene. For a CU, he shoots the windshield area, so that the audience cannot help noticing the leather seats inside and the gleaming surface of the hood.

Now Ross admires the car, but he admires Pam even more; he happens to be her boy friend. He wants to open the sequence closer to Pam at the car, so he shoots *his* LS from where Roscoe took his medium shot. Being a good cameraman, he includes enough of the background to show the pleasant setting. Next, Ross takes his MS from where Roscoe took his closeup, framing it so that Pam really dominates the shot more than the windshield area. Then for his CU, he shoots Pam's hand wearing the friendship ring he has given her.

Roscoe and Ross have shot relatively different sequences, both perfectly acceptable. Good continuity was applied in each case, even though the stories differed in emphasis.

Every moviewise cameraman, by the way, will use an actor or actors (good-looking ones are always desirable!) to give life and visual appeal to a scene even when they are not the true subject of the movie. Furthermore, they can, by appropriate position or action, draw the audience eye to a detail the cameraman wants to be noticed.

THE EXTREME LONG SHOT

Thus the simple sequence develops and its basic elements reveal themselves to be flexible and elastic. The elasticity can be considerable. The long shot, for instance, can become very long, producing the *extreme long shot* or "ELS," which gives *a far distant view of the area in which action takes place.*

Extreme Long Shot   Long Shot

In a true ELS, it is not the action that dominates the screen, but the *distance* from the action; or the *surroundings* in which the action takes place. In the ELS of the church it is only a modest part of the scene.

ELS's are often used solely to establish the physical character of a location or to render its distinctive atmosphere. This usage is a common way of opening many films—aerial shots of a city to show its skyscrapers, tenements or teeming traffic; sweeping landscape shots of forests and mountains to convey their grandeur and loneliness; mist-shrouded views of a castle on a remote headland to convey its isolation and suggest mystery or menace.[8]

THE EXTREME CLOSEUP

The *extreme closeup* or "ECU"[9] is at the opposite end of the scale from the ELS. It magnifies the closeup, bringing it even closer to the eye. The subject often fills the screen, even extending beyond its borders. The ECU is used for dramatic emphasis or to show up details that might not be clearly seen in a closeup.

Closeup   *Extreme Closeup*

Suppose you are hired to shoot a wedding anniversary party. One of the sequences shows the husband presenting his wife with a ring to mark the occasion. You have moved in with long and medium shots to a closeup of the wife admiring her present. Your audience—especially the women in it—would like a closer look at the ring. So you have the wife hold up her hand and you bring your camera in very close for an ECU. When projected, the shot shows the many facets of the stone in sparkling detail big on the screen.

Relativity of subject matter applies to the extreme closeup, too. If you are filming a locomotive in a station, an ultra-close shot of one of the huge wheels becomes as much of an ECU as wife's ring.

THE FULL-FIGURE SHOT[10]

What of the medium shot? It cannot go to any extreme in the direction of long shot or closeup without falling into the category of one or the other. Compared to them, it is pretty limited in range. Very often it takes the form of the most limiting of all motion-picture shots, the *full-figure shot*. The full-figure shot is self-explanatory, and needs no definition. It is relative. It may be made of an adult or child, an elephant or a cat, or an inanimate object like a lighthouse. However, to get a full-figure shot of the lighthouse, the cameraman would have to back off to a long shot—another example of relativity.

Three Examples of the
Full-Figure Shot

The full-figure shot usually has a little head-and-foot room to show a trace of background, whereas in the ordinary MS, the lower portion of the figure is frequently cut off once the LS has established it.

SUMMARY

The LS, MS, and CU are strictly relative. Distances between them are determined by the nature of action and location, by the cameraman's personal preference, and by what he wants to emphasize to his audience.

• The basic elements are elastic. The long shot may stretch to the extreme long shot, or location shot; the closeup may contract to the extreme sloseup. The medium shot, however, has little range and becomes very sharply limited in the full-figure shot.

CHAPTER 3

THE REESTABLISHING SHOT

CONNECTING SEQUENCES

We have observed that a single sequence such as the sales call on Mr. Producer will give you a "motion picture" as long as you apply the basic elements of continuity to it. But most of the movies you shoot will be too rich in action to be told in just one sequence. Suppose his secretary came to his desk, thereby introducing something new into the scene. Remember that as you finished your simple sequence of Mr. Producer, you were taking the closeup. Your audience would be unable to see the secretary unless you—the cameraman—enabled it to. Thus you must have another sequence to introduce her and to tell her part in the story. Still more sequences will follow, as new actors and new action are added to the story.

Almost all action breaks down into a series of related sequences. They may be considered as the links of a chain. The links, to make a chain, must be joined; the sequences, to form a coherent motion-picture story, must be tied together. Coherence is obtained through good continuity, and for good continuity properly tied motion-picture sequences are indispensable.

One of the continuity devices that joins sequences together is called a *reestablishing shot,* or "RS." It is a medium or long shot that gets its name from the fact that it usually follows a closeup and *again establishes the general scene* much as the original LS established it in the beginning.

So, in the case in point, you *pull back* far enough with your camera in order that your next shot may show the general scene again, with the secretary actually entering it. Your audience is instantly oriented with regard to her entrance; it understands that *she came from somewhere* beyond the screen boundary and did not magically pop up beside Mr. Producer. Now you can go ahead and shoot the second sequence with the secretary in it.[11]

There are other methods of reestablishing besides the pull back. These will be discussed a little later in this chapter.

Bear in mind that the prime purpose of reestablishing the old scene is to carry action smoothly into a new sequence. Such action may take place either in the old physical setting or in a new one. Your second sequence began with a reestablishing shot showing the secretary entering the office and then going through the action of taking dictation from Mr. Producer.[12] Your third sequence could take place in her own office—a new location—to show her typing out the dictation. The RS necessary to connect the second and third sequences would show the secretary leaving the boss's office to enter her own.

So you reestablish whenever a new subject, live or inanimate, is introduced into the story; or when the subject moves from an old location to a new one.

REESTABLISHING THE OLD

You should also reestablish when you *reintroduce* people or action that has already been established, but which has been off the screen for a while.

Suppose you're asked to make a movie story about the Howell family shoving off for a run in their cabin cruiser. You establish the overall scene in a long shot showing the boys, Jeffrey and Jim, at the fore and aft lines, ready to cast off. Their mother supervises while their sister Jill watches from the comfort of the cabin. (Dad isn't in the scene for the simple reason that he is serving as the cameraman!)

Next, you shoot a medium shot to provide a closer view of the overall action as the boys start to untie the lines.

It would be impossible to shoot a closeup of the combined action because of the distance that separates Jeffrey and Jim. Besides, each one is performing a slightly different action. So you come in first for a CU of Jeffrey removing the bow line from the piling. This close angle excludes Jim at the stern of the boat. Now when Jeffrey completes his action, you want to show Jim removing the stern line from the cleat. So you shoot a reestablishing shot showing Jim in the background.

This example sharply points out a fundamental difference between motion picture and still picture photography and the difficulty of illustrating motion picture action with still pictures! In the still picture used here, Jim is barely discernible. In motion pictures, however, Jim's movement in the background would be more than enough to reestablish him.

To complete the sequence, move in to shoot an MS of Jim at work with mother watching, then a CU of the action and finally, an ECU as mother's hand takes the line aboard.

The action of casting off is completed. Now you want to show the boys pushing the boat free of the dock—a completely new action. So you return to a longer angle to reestablish them both as they push off and jump aboard.

You can end your movie with a final LS that shows the boat moving out on the river or you can add still more sequences before the closing shot, example—Jim moving to the wheel and starting the engine, *as long as you reestablish with each new action.*

THE REESTABLISHING SHOT

Establishing Shot (LS)   Medium Shot
Medium Shot   Closeup
Closeup   Extreme Closeup
Reestablishing Shot   Reestablishing Shot

The frequent use of reestablishing shots is necessary to refresh the audience's memory of the scene, and to remind it of the relationship of the parts to the whole—of how the boys' individual actions relate to the overall action of getting the boat under way. It is a continuity truism that an audience, always looking ahead to what is coming, *rarely keeps in mind more than one scene prior to the one it is looking at.* It must periodically be reminded of how a small scene fits into the larger scene that includes it.

Remember that the human eye unconsciously refuses to look at too many closeups in succession, and reorients itself every now and then by a quick look around. Let your camera do likewise for your audience by frequently reestablishing the scene, otherwise confusion may kill interest.

You reestablish, therefore, not only to tie sequences together, but also to keep your audience from getting lost.

REESTABLISHING BY PULLING BACK

There are three customary ways of making a reestablishing shot. We have already used one in our explanation: *pulling back,* the simplest method. The other two are *panning* and the *reverse-angle shot.* All three methods can frequently be applied to the same story. Let us take one example for all three and see how it works out.

Your good friend and neighbor, Mr. Montgomery, is going to provide you with your action. Montgomery, who is a stickler for proper inflation in his automobile tires, is outdoors checking their air pressure with a gauge.

Using what you have learned so far, you make a movie of this action. You take an LS from across the street showing the car parked in front of the house and Neighbor Montgomery standing beside the left rear tire. Your MS follows from a position in the middle of the street and advances the action: it shows Montgomery kneeling to apply the gauge to the tire valve. Finally, in your CU, he is actually applying the gauge to the valve and reading the pressure. (An ECU showing just the gauge and the reading on it would be logical—but optional—at this point.)

You have now completed your first sequence. Next, Mr. Montgomery rises, walks over to the left front tire, and repeats his performance. This separate action constitutes a separate sequence, and therefore you must reestablish in order to tie it to the first sequence.

The first method of reestablishing is to *pull back* to a medium- or long-shot position, whichever is back far enough to include both the rear tire, the location from which Montgomery is *coming,* and the front tire, the location to which he is *going.* Then you move in again for medium and closeup shots of him at the front tire.

REESTABLISHING BY PANNING

The second method of reestablishing is by *panning* (derived from the word "panorama"). After pulling back from the closeup, the camera is panned to *follow* the action as it moves from one location to another.

You would pan Mr. Montgomery by following him through the camera's

SIMPLE SEQUENCE

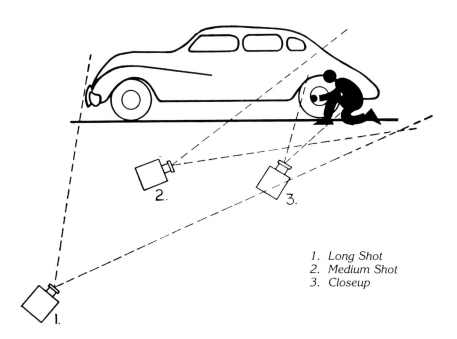

1. Long Shot
2. Medium Shot
3. Closeup

REESTABLISHING BY PULLING BACK

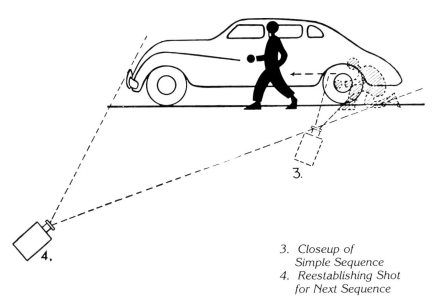

3. Closeup of
   Simple Sequence
4. Reestablishing Shot
   for Next Sequence

REESTABLISHING BY PANNING

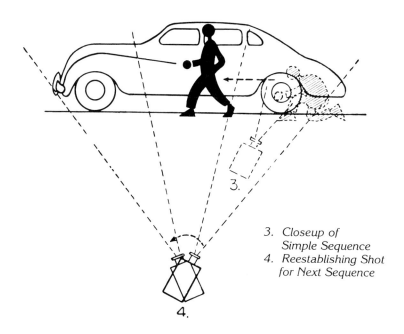

3. Closeup of
   Simple Sequence
4. Reestablishing Shot
   for Next Sequence

REESTABLISHING BY REVERSE ANGLE

3. Closeup of Simple Sequence
4. Reestablishing Shot for Next Sequence
5. Reverse Angle of 4

viewfinder as he moved from the rear to the front tire, carrying your audience along fron one point to another.

So much can be said on the subject of the pan that, now we have explained its use as a reestablishing shot, we are going to postpone further discussion until Chapter 8 where we can go more thoroughly into the various aspects of handling this sometimes troublesome shot.

REESTABLISHING WITH THE REVERSE ANGLE

Now we proceed to a third method of reestablishing—the *reverse-angle shot.*

To get a reverse angle, you reposition your camera to shoot in the opposite direction. There are always two shots involved in reestablishing by reverse angle; there must be a preceding shot to provide the angle from which the switch to reverse is made.

To illustrate: you shoot the sequence of Mr. Montgomery checking the rear tire as you did before. Now move the camera to a position directly behind him and the rear tire. As he rises and moves away, your film or video camera shoots past him down the length of the car to the front tire.

For the next sequence, you reposition the camera behind the front tire and shoot back toward the rear one. You show your performer moving *away* from the rear tire and *toward* the front tire, giving you a reverse angle shot.

If you check the drawing for "Reestablishing by Reverse Angle," you will note that Camera Position No. 4 is designated as the reestablishing shot, not No. 5, the reverse angle. Don't let this confuse you. The No. 4 angle alone can serve as the reestablishing shot if you showed Mr. Montgomery moving *all the way* from the rear to the front tire. But then this would amount to just another *pull back* from a different angle! It is the addition of the reverse angle, No. 5, that creates a new method of reestablishing.[13]

Varying your reestablishing shots will enrich your sequences pictorially and avoid monotony. Be guided by story needs—and by good sense.

SUMMARY

All action breaks down into motion-picture sequences.

• A new sequence is necessary wherever a new subject, live or inanimate, is introduced into the picture, or when the subject is moved from an old to a new location.

• In order to join motion-picture sequences together, the reestablishing shot is used.

• The RS not only ties sequences together but also keeps the audience from getting confused or lost.

• There are three ways to reestablish: by pulling back, by panning, and by shooting from a reverse angle.

CHAPTER 4

OVERLAP AND MATCHING ACTION

CURING JUMPY ACTION

Good continuity demands a smooth, uninterrupted flow of action from one shot to the next. That impression of smoothness is destroyed for the audience when there are sudden gaps in the movement of screen actors between shots.

If, returning to our opening example, your first shot of Mr. Producer was an LS showing him starting to rise from his chair and your next shot an MS of him standing erect, the audience may be conscious of an irritating jump in the action, as though a few feet of film showing Mr. Producer going through the act of rising had been cut out.

This jumpy action[14] is hard on the audience's eyes—and harder on your reputation as a cameraman. A cure is *overlap.* Defining this brand new term, we say that overlap is the reshooting of action that took place at *the tail end of the preceding shot.*

Suppose you're shooting a boy meets girl story—Karl and Karen getting together over two bottles of Coke. You start in MS position to establish them and shoot the action of Karen raising the bottle to her lips and taking a healthy swallow. At this point you stop the camera and move in for a closeup of Karen.

But before you start your CU, you ask Karen to repeat the final action of the medium shot. From CU position, you begin shooting as she once again raises the bottle and drinks; then continue with new action in the CU as she puts down the bottle.

Stop for a moment and look at what you have done. If you screen your footage, you will see that you have two shots, from different positions, showing identical action. This is the footage that comprises the overlap.

Now with your finished movie, as you want the audience to see it, you are obviously not going to show both pieces of action in their entirety. This sort of repetition would be worse from an audience's point of view than a gap in the action. So avoid it when editing by performing an operation known as *matching action.* In film, as you will see in the next sequence, this involves cut-

MATCHING ACTION
Between Shots

Closeups
(Below)

Medium Shots
(Above)

Reestablishing Shot

ting out redundant footage. However, you don't physically cut videotape since the spliced tape can cause a glitch or roll between scenes; it can also damage the equipment. You get rid of the superfluous footage by simply omitting it when you re-record during the editing process. (See Chapter 13, sequence on "When The Shooting Is Over: Editing Videotape.")

HOW TO MATCH ACTION

To match action in the overlap of Karen when editing, you pick the film frames in your MS footage and the frames in your CU footage where the action is most identical. Those are the frames in which Karen is actually drinking the Coke.

You discard everything that *comes after* these frames in the MS, and everything that comes *before* the identical frames in the CU. Then you splice the two shots together.

The frames where Karen is drinking the Coke serve your purpose best because it is easiest to match action at a point in the film where the action is comparatively slow. As you gain experience and deftness in editing, however, you should always match action *on motion,* such as the point where Karen is either putting the bottle in her mouth or removing it. A much smoother transition between scenes results, inasmuch as the audience's eye is busy following movement, instead of pausing at a static point in the action.

The video cameraman can try to match action without overlap by starting his MS at precisely the point in the action where the CU stops but we can't guarantee there won't be a slight jump in the action. The solution is to apply the General Rule. Chapter 6 will tell you all about that.

The human eye watching Karen does not need overlap because, unlike the camera which stops shooting when you change distance or angle, it does not stop looking at Karen even while its owner moves around. By using overlap, the audience eye may also look at her without being made conscious of interruptions while camera positions are being changed.

There is a second example of overlap in the illustrations for matching action. Note that the final picture is a two-shot reestablishing Karl with Karen. In the transition from CU back to MS, you should shoot overlapping footage again. In this case, the overlap in each shot is Karen's action in putting the bottle down.

WATCH OUT FOR DISCREPANCIES

In shooting matching action, you must be careful to avoid discrepancies between shots. If you didn't notice any discrepancies, look again. Note that in the first CU of Karen, the level of the Coke is below the neck of the bottle. In the reestablishing shot, however, the level has dropped almost half-way! Obviously, Karen took other sips from the bottle after the CU was completed and before the reestablishing two-shot was begun.

This is one of those little slips in continuity that destroys the credibility of the action on film since it is supposed to be continuous; and which sharp-eyed audiences delight in finding in elaborately produced feature film. It is why, in professional productions, an assistant is on the scene to catch discrepancies before they are permanently fixed in the final version of the movie. If you haven't someone alert on hand to fill the role, you, as cameraman, must be your own script person.

However, the cameraman could have saved this situation even after Karen took that additional sip. He could have concealed the discrepancy before shooting his reestablishing shot by having Karen wrap her fingers around the upper part of the bottle to hide the lowered level. Using a subterfuge like this is aptly called "cheating." Cheat shots are perfectly acceptable as long as they work. They may even be a challenge to the ingenuity of the cameraman, although we don't recommend looking for them!

Perhaps your detective instinct has been whetted and you may have noted what seems to be another discrepancy about the level in the Coke bottle. Karl's bottle was full in the establishing two-shot but partly empty in the reestablishing shot, but we didn't see him drink any of the coke. Discrepancy? No. Karl was *offscreen* during the closeup of Karen. Therefore an audience would naturally assume he had imbibed some of his drink while he was absent from the screen.

Discrepancies—"discontinuities" is another apt term—are characteristic movie gremlins that gnaw bits out of pictorial continuity. They can pop up anywhere between sequences as well as between shots—especially if you shoot parts of your story out of sequence. They also try to creep into the most ordinary action. Eye movement is a common example. Look at those closeups of Karen. It would have been a typical gremlin act of mischief had she looked directly at the camera instead of in the direction of Karl offscreen. Don't blame your actor or actress if this happens, as it often does. You're the director as well as cameraman; it's up to you to keep it from happening. How do you avoid it? Stay alert!

CONTROLLED AND UNCONTROLLED ACTION

You can readily see that for a cameraman to shoot overlap, he must be able to *control* the action so that his subject will repeat it at the beginning of the next shot.

This is no problem for the moviemaker who is using professional actors or actresses who are accustomed to taking direction. Even the cameraman shooting for fun will be able to control action as long as his subjects are responsive to his orders, for example, the family at home eating Sunday dinner or vacation friends romping on a beach.

If the action cannot be controlled—if the subject is a four-alarm fire, a sports event such as a tennis match or baby romping in playpen—you can still shoot overlap by using more than one camera operated by friends or colleagues.

If there are only two cameras, the best solution is to assign one to take both the LS and MS shots, and the other to do just the CU work. Overlap then occurs only on the MS and CU shots, but this is the most efficient compromise, since once your scene has been established you are bound to use more MS than LS shots.[15]

The ideal situation would be to have three cameras stationed at LS, MS and CU positions. To get overlap, first roll the LS camera, then start the MS *before* stopping the LS, and begin the CU *before* ending the MS shot.

In practice, however, this sort of control is difficult to achieve. It may simply be more practical to roll all three cameras simultaneously throughout the entire length of the sequence. The complete action will then be registered on three separate lengths of film or videotape, each shot from a different position: one, entirely a long shot; another, a medium shot; and the third, a closeup.

This lavishness in shooting footage gives you the potential for overlap *throughout* the sequence. You will be able, when editing, to go back and forth anywhere in your story, matching action between the different shots. The possibilities for visual variety are self-evident.

We are loath to urge such a three-camera setup on the home cameraman or student shooting film. It is difficult and a lot of work. We do not recommend it to the nonprofessional video cameraman. The editing problems are too complex for his skills and equipment.

However, a multi-camera setup is often necessary in the professional worlds of visual media when the subject is a one-time-only event—a championship boxing match or the destruction of a costly set in a feature film. These never-to-be-repeated scenes virtually demand several cameras running simultaneously from different positions and angles to assure complete coverage. This method has added advantages when a tight shooting schedule prevails, as in making entertainment movies for television. It not only saves shooting time, but preserves the feeling of spontaneity in the actors' performances.

There is no concern about overlap in a professional, multi-video camera setup in either a television studio or in the field with a mobile TV control truck. The director, even when he's using a half-dozen cameras or more to cover a sports event like football, can cut *instantaneously* from one camera to another without any jump in the action by using a video switcher.[16]

Although overlap should usually be considered a "must" by the cameraman, occasions will arise when it will be impossible to match action between shots. Suppose the action is uncontrolled and only one camera is available? This is usually the case when shooting a movie at home. It is a situation often faced by the TV news cameraman. Only a single cameraman is usually sent out to cover the average news story.

Fortunately, there is more than one solution to this problem. One answer is in the use of *cut-aways,* which will be described in the next chapter; the other answer is in *the general rule,* the subject of Chapter 6.

SUMMARY

Jumpy action destroys that impression of smoothness between shots in a sequence which is a mark of good continuity.

• Overlap is a cure for jumpy action. It is the reshooting of action that has taken place at the tail end of the previous scene.

• Overlap makes possible the matching of action between successive film shots by picking frames in each where the action is identical, regardless of a difference in angle or distance from the subject. Videotape cannot use overlap; superfluous footage is omitted when re-recording during the editing process.

• Overlap can be made by the individual cameraman when the action is controlled. When the action is uncontrolled, overlap is possible through the use of additional cameras.

• In the case of never-to-be-repeated scenes, it pays to run several cameras simultaneously from various positions throughout the entire action, so that the editor can cut between LS, MS, and CU anywhere in the movie.

• When the action is uncontrolled and only one camera is available, jumpy action can be avoided by the use of cut-aways and the general rule.

CHAPTER 5

SECONDARY SHOTS

INCIDENTAL BUT INDISPENSABLE SHOTS

We are making headway in our study of pictorial continuity. We have taken note of the structure of the sequence, of how sequences are connected, and of how those connections are made smoother and more interesting to an audience. So far we have an outline, a skeleton form of continuity.

We now take a look at certain shots which will serve to develop that outline, add flesh to the skeleton of continuity.

These are shots *in addition to* the LS, MS, and CU which carry the main action of the sequence. Such incidental shots are known as *cut-ins* and *cut-aways.* They are brief shots, and are usually closeups and extreme closeups, or occasionally medium—or even long—shots.

Cut-ins and cut-aways are among the most versatile devices in continuity, useful in many ways, rich in material. They are incidental but indispensable, as vital to the proper operation of a movie as ball bearings are to the wheels of an automobile.

THE CUT-IN

The cut-in derives its name from the fact that it *cuts into the main action.* Suppose you're shooting a classic Western scene—a confrontation between sheriff and gunslinger. You show an MS of the latter starting to draw, then a CU of his hand pulling his gun from its holster. The CU is a cut-in. Or if your subject is an actor packing his bags in a hotel room and you want to show how widely travelled he is, shoot ECUs of the many hotel labels on his bags. Each ECU is a cut-in. You are also using cut-ins if, in a home movie of two boys—Johnny and Freddy—taking a dog for a walk, you shoot an ECU of Johnny's hand snapping the leash onto the dog collar, or a CU of the dog's legs as it trots off.

THE CUT-IN AND CUT-AWAY

Top to Bottom

Establishing Shot   *Cut-in*
Medium Shot   *Cut-away*
Closeup   *Reestablishing Shot*

THE CUT-AWAY

The cut-away is categorically opposite to the cut-in. It does not cut into the main action, but *cuts away to a related subject or to a separate action that is going on at the same time.*

The sequences with which we illustrated the cut-in also provide examples of the cut-away. In the sheriff-gunslinger sequence, a cut-away would be an MS of townpeople watching the scene; in the packing sequence, a CU of a porter waiting for the bags would be a cut-away; in the home movie, a CU of Freddy watching Johnny put on the leash would also be a cut-away.

However, a cut-away need not be connected to the main action in the *same time or space frame.* We definitely have a cut-away if we dissolve to a memory sequence by the sheriff in which he has a similar confrontation with a different gunslinger in another town at some earlier time; or if we dissolved from the porter in the hotel room to a scene of him at home making love to his wife to indicate what he'd much rather be doing!

Do not confuse the cut-in with the cut-away. The cut-away is far more important and you will use it much more often. It is a vital tool in the editing room to resolve problems of poor continuity such as jumpy action. Indeed many professional movie makers plan their cut-aways before shooting. They are invaluable as protection shots and to bridge sequences of noncontinuous action.

A thought to bear in mind about the cut-away is that the main action should be established before the cut-away is used. In other words, there should be a visual reference point preceding the cut-away.

In our last illustration we suggested a shot of Freddy as a cut-away. It is important that Freddy should have been seen in an earlier shot, in an LS, for example. Even though he may be merely a background figure in that shot, his presence has been established onscreen, and the audience is neither surprised or confused when he appears later by himself in a cut-away.[17]

(On the other hand, it is not necessary to establish cut-ins, because a cut-in is part of the main action and is therefore automatically established in one of the main shots of the sequence.)

The practice of visually establishing cut-ins and cut-aways has its exceptions like so many other practices of good continuity. It is sometimes ignored in highly specialized film or video forms such as television news stories or documentaries. These forms are extremely economical of footage; entire sequences may consist of a mixture of unestablished cut-ins and cut-aways. Such stories depend strongly on *narration* to tie the shots together and give them meaning.

HEAD-ON AND TAIL-AWAY SHOTS

Other secondary shots are the "head-on" and "tail-away." They are neither as frequently used nor are as important as cut-ins and cut-aways, but when called for, their use imparts a dynamic visual quality.

The head-on is simply a shot of the action *directly approaching* the camera. It is coming "head-on" or "full-face." Johnny and his friend walking directly toward the camera would be a head-on. This type of shot is often used as a genuine LS in order to introduce a sequence.

The directness of the head-on can give it a strong dramatic quality. One of the punchiest shots in motion pictures is the repeatedly used head-on approach of an auto, tank, horses, or marching men, shot from ground level, and showing the moving subject passing directly overhead.

HEAD-ON AND TAIL-AWAY

Head-on Shot   Tail-away Shot

The *tail-away* is the exact opposite of the head-on shot, and depicts action from the rear as it moves *away* from the camera. If you shoot the action of Johnny walking down the street with his friend and the dog from the rear, with the subjects moving away from the camera, you have a tail-away.[18]

This shot is popular for ending a sequence. The movement of a subject away from the camera, its decrease in size as it recedes, strongly suggest that the action in the sequence is completed, whether it's Johnny and friend walking away or a cowboy galloping off to the horizon.

INSERTS

Inserts are secondary shots which emphasize specific visual information or serve to heighten dramatic impact in the main action.[19] They also help an editor take the curse off awkward continuity. Inserts are usually close shots—CUs and ECUs—and can be of practically anything—the hand pointing the gun at Mr. Producer, the contract he is reading, his pen as it signs your first check.

Frequently they are cut-ins and cut-aways. The cut-in of Johnny's hand snapping the leash onto the dog collar is an insert. So is a cut-in of the dog's moving legs as it chases after a stick Johnny throws on the lawn. The same scene provides us with inserts that are cut-aways—a CU of the stick lying on the grass or Johnny's smiling face as he watches the dog offscreen.

Inserts can play a key role in transitions between sequences. Examples are the classic clichés of falling calendar leaves or the moving hands of a clock to denote the passage of time. They also offer a succinct method of plot development. We've all seen movies in which a succession of close shots of different newspaper headlines convey information that advances the plot.

Sometimes inserts are unrelated in continuity but are placed together during editing to project a common idea. (This so-called *montage* is discussed in greater detail in the chapter on buildup). A series of single shots of a sprinter, a high jumper, a pole vaulter and a shotput thrower in action readily projects the idea of a track and field meet.

In a commercial film production, when the story has several insert shots, they are usually set aside to be filmed consecutively at one time; then edited into the movie. Such a consolidation can be more economical of time and effort that shooting the inserts individually as they come up in the story. It's possible the term "insert" derives from such a procedure. Of course the home cameraman can follow the same procedure when shooting the inserts for his story.

Unfortunately, this convenience is not for the videotape cameraman/editor who does not have access to electronic editing equipment. Without it, the difficulty of getting cleanly edited videotape is such that it pays to shoot inserts, especially cut-aways, in the exact order in which the audience will see them onscreen. (See Chapter 13, "When The Shooting Is Over: Editing Videotape"). This is not as bad as it may seem. In the story of Johnny and the dog, the cut-in of the snap-on leash can easily be shot in sequence since the action is controlled. That's true also of the cut-aways of Johnny's face and the stick. When you shoot the cut-in of the dog's moving legs (it'll probably take several throws of the stick to get this shot), don't forget to make a reestablishing shot of the dog running.

WIDER USES OF CUT-INS AND CUT-AWAYS

This chapter provides little more than an introduction to cut-ins and cut-aways. Our purpose at this point is only to define and describe these very important shots. We will have more to say about them very soon, notably in the chapters on directional continuity and buildup where we will show to what varied uses they lend themselves.

SUMMARY

Cut-ins and cut-aways are among the most useful shots in pictorial continuity. They are secondary shots, incidental to the main action. They are usually CUs and ECUs although sometimes they may be a longer shot.

• The cut-in gets its name from the fact that it cuts into the main action; whereas the cut-away does exactly the opposite and cuts away to a related subject on at the same time.

• The main action to which the cut-away relates should be visually established before the cut-away is used.

• The head-on and tail-away are other secondary shots. The head-on is a shot of action directly approaching the camera; the tail-away depicts the action from the rear as it moves away from the camera.

• Inserts are secondary shots which emphasize visual detail and so are usually CUs and ECUs. They are frequently cut-ins and cut-aways. To expedite shooting, inserts are often shot out of sequence and placed in proper continuity during editing.

• Cut-ins and cut-aways have varied uses which will be described in future chapters.

CHAPTER 6

THE GENERAL RULE

A REAL MUST

So vital to smooth continuity is the avoidance or minimizing of jumpy action that we are going to do something we haven't done before—lay down a hard-and-fast rule which *must* be followed.

We call it *the general rule,* because it is applied to all the shots of a motion-picture sequence, without exception, consistently, *generally.*

The general rule states: When shooting a new scene, change the size of the image, or change the angle, or both.

We dislike the word "must"; the technique of pictorial continuity is so highly flexible, so much depends on the imaginative spark of the individual cameraman, that we prefer to use the word "should" even when we strongly feel something ought to be done. But there is no such qualification as "should" for the general rule. As its name unmistakably implies, it is used everywhere; it must be and can be.

It can be done by you as cameraman while shooting a sequence, or by you as editor when editing (by using cut-ins and cut-aways; but remember that you, as the editor cannot put into the movie something you as the cameraman left out, so take those extra shots!).

Why all the fuss about a change of image size or of angle with every new shot? The reasons are two: the first is the fact that this simple operation always makes it possible to cover up any jump in the action because the audience's attention will be taken up by the "something different, something new" created by the change; and the second reason is to achieve visual variety, for which the general rule is the basic, unfailing means.

OUTWITTING JUMPY ACTION FROM THE FLANK

All this to-do about the general rule's covering up jumpy action will not, we hope, cause you to hesitate about applying it. Truth is, you have been using it from the very beginning; you have been changing the size of the image every time you moved from the long shot to medium shot, from medium shot to closeup. You did it in the movie sequence on Mr. Producer, as well as Karen drinking the coke. And this is how we got around the problem of the jumpy action of baby in the playpen in Chapter 4, when we changed the type of shot from an MS to a CU.

Overlap eliminates jumpy action by overpowering it with a frontal attack, so to speak. The general rule outwits it by a deceptive play around the flanks. The best solution is a "combined operation" where both overlap and the general rule can be employed. But let us take a case where overlap is impossible—where the action cannot be controlled and where there is only one camera at work—to see how the general rule can be most useful and most necessary.

You have certainly seen the work of a cameraman who starts to shoot a scene, stops the camera in order to save footage until something more interesting develops, then starts shooting again without changing position or lens. The result is an inevitable jump between shots which is hard on the audience's eye and classifies the cameraman immediately as an awkward novice.

Take, for example, that popular sequence of a child climbing the steps of a slide. Proud Dad began to shoot when little sister Betty was clambering up the first few steps; as she moved slowly from step to step, Dad began to wonder whether he wasn't wasting footage on this slow, repetitious movement, so he stopped the camera when Betty was about halfway up. Then, as she got to the final step, he started his camera again *without changing position* and caught her as she triumphantly scrambled over onto the top of the slide.

On-screen, to all appearances, Betty has literally jumped from the middle steps to the top rung. It is a remarkable performance, but more suitable to a television "Bionic Baby" than to a family movie.

Now you shoot the sequence the right way, by applying the general rule. You'll find that you can be just as economical in respect to footage. Here's how you do it.

You start with Betty on the first steps, and you stop your camera as before, when she has reached the half-way mark. But instead of staying in the same position for your next shot, you move in for an MS—make it a full-figure—as she continues her climb. Finally, a closeup catches Betty's gleeful expression as she comes up the last step. You can reestablish as Betty pulls herself onto the slide itself.

In this example you change the image size by *enlarging* it when you move the camera closer to the subject with the MS and the CU. In the RS you would change the image size by pulling back and *decreasing* it.

You can see how a change of image size creates a *different* scene, gives you something right at the beginning to attract the audience's attention so that it will overlook a jump in the action. Although it is aware that Betty has traveled

THE GENERAL RULE

No Change of Image Size
or Angle

Change of Image Size Only
   Long Shot
   Medium Shot
   Closeup

some distance between the original LS and the RS, its eye has not been irritated, nor has its sense of logic been disturbed. The new approach the camera has taken toward its subject by a change of image size stimulates the audience, whose imagination cheerfully carries it through the unimportant action the camera has chosen to ignore.

The "something different" provided by the general rule, that variety which gives novelty to each shot and stimulates audience interest afresh, is a quality some cameramen consider even more important than the fact that the rule can cover up a jump in the action.

They contend that variety soothes the audience's eye, which is bound to tire if it looks at the same scene too long. Equally important, they believe the constant change to something different and interesting gives the motion picture a snap and movement it must have to be really good.

At any rate, regardless of which you consider the more important, you have two excellent reasons why you must use the general rule.

ANGLES

Changing the image size is one way of putting the general rule into operation. A change of angle can smooth over a jump in the action or provide variety just as effectively, at times even better.

Angles provide infinite opportunities for attaining that "something different," opportunities which can be tremendously exciting and dramatic. Consider just one minor example—Betty making that epic stair climb. Instead of just changing your image size, you change angles with every shot in the sequence. Your LS is the same, but the MS is taken from the side looking up, and the CU is slightly off from a ninety-degree angle at eye level, while your final RS is a reverse angle. There is no question but that you have greatly increased the interest and animation of the sequence.

There is no need to make a choice between changing image size and changing the angle when shooting a new scene. There is no conflict, for the two work hand in hand and one improves the other. The two should be used together whenever possible. Remember the general rule: When shooting a new scene, change the image size, or change the angle, *or both.*

LENS CHANGES

So far you have changed the image size only by moving toward or away from your subject, using just the normal[20] lens in your camera. But you can also change image size—make it larger or smaller—*without moving your camera,* by using lenses of different focal lengths. These may be *long (telephoto), wide-angle,* or a *zoom* which is a multi-focal length lens.

If you buy a personal camera today, it will probably have a zoom lens as standard equipment. The zoom combines the functions of the normal, the wide-angle, and the long or telephoto lens. The long lens enlarges the image size; the wide-angle decreases it.

A popular zoom lens on the 16mm camera ranges from 12mm (wide-angle) to 120mm (long), giving you a choice of any focal length inbetween. A long lens setting of 50mm will double the size of the image set at 25mm; a wide-angle setting of 15mm will decrease the image size by almost half that of 25mm.[21] This flexibility of lens changes is a great advantage when you want to adjust the framing of a shot with speed and precision.

Professional video cameras come equipped with zoom lenses with ratios varying from 10:1 to 17:1, although some studio cameras have ratios of 40:1 or more. Home cameras have smaller ratios, such as 6:1.

Separate lenses for telephoto and wide-angle shots called *fixed lenses* long predated the zoom and are still in use, although mainly in commercial production.

THE GENERAL RULE
Change of Image Size and Angle

Establishing Shot   *Closeup*

Medium Shot   *Reestablishing Shot*

There are few situations in which the general rule cannot be applied with a camera equipped only with an ordinary lens and moved around by the cameraman. Nonetheless, it must be granted that by eliminating the need for physical movement, the long, wide-angle and zoom lens in particular, make the cameraman's task much easier and save a great deal of time as well.

CAVEATS ABOUT LENSES

However, every good thing has its price. Cameramen using other than normal lenses must be very careful about their effect on perspective. A long lens, or a zoom used as a long lens, pulls the background unnaturally close to the subject, flattens the perspective and requires careful attention to focus.

The distortion of perspective can be especially dangerous when the subject of the story is seen in line with one or more objects in the background, such as a chimney or tree. With an ordinary lens, there is no noticeable distortion of perspective. There is enough distance between the human figure in the foreground and a tree in the background, even though the two are in line, so that the tree is a remote, undistracting detail, hardly noticed by the viewer. On the other hand, a long lens, by foreshortening the distance between the nearer and farther objects, will bring the background tree so close to the foreground figure that the tree trunk seems to be sprouting from the person's head!

Sometimes a cameraman will go for this foreshortening deliberately in order to create a spectacular visual effect. You can do this yourself at a baseball game by using a long lens in a shot from behind home plate taking in both pitcher and batter. When the pitcher hurls the ball, his outflung arm seems to come right up to the batter and the ball within inches of his face! This is admittedly a stunt shot and does nothing in itself to further the aim of good continuity, but it has tremendous audience impact.

And there are occasions when the cameraman has no choice—he *must* use his zoom as a long lens in order to get the shot. A normal lens just won't do the job because camera movement with it is so impractical or simply impossible. This is the case when shooting a football game from the stands or when filming objects at great distances, such as a mountain peak from across a valley.

Their greater power of magnification makes long or telephoto lenses very desirable for CUs or ECUs when the subject is nearby but close approach is impossible. This is often the case in zoos or exhibit halls; or when the cameraman must operate from behind police lines set up to guard a celebrity. And even when a subject is accessible, it may be possible to get the picture only if one keeps one's distance and uses a long lens. When shooting wild life a close approach might scare the subject away, and this applies equally to human beings—whether children or politicians—whose awareness of the cameraman often makes them freeze in self-consciousness or else "mug" the camera to the ruination of a natural picture.

Only make sure your camera is rock-steady when using a long lens, especially if your subject is a considerable distance away. Otherwise, because of the highly magnified image, any vibration or other unsteadiness of the camera—even if its movement is slight—may cause the subject to jump out of frame or be distractingly unsteady. The longer the focal length, the greater the possibility of this happening. So give your telephoto lens firm support when you shoot.

Sometimes the matter of accessibility works in reverse. Instead of being too far away, you find yourself too close for a normal lens to take in all you want to photograph. Physical limitations within doors, or outdoors on a narrow street, may make it impossible for you to back off far enough to get everything in. The solution to this problem is the wide-angle lens which gives your camera a much greater angle. A wide-angle lens used in a small room gives a surprising sense of spaciousness.

Nonetheless think of shooting your story primarily with the normal lens, as your eye would see the scene. Save the other lens uses for the real visual needs of your story. Don't—please don't—use the zoom just because it's there. Pity the poor audience that has to watch the work of a "zoom-happy" cameraman!

SUMMARY

The one rule of pictorial continuity that can and *must* invariably be used is the so-called general rule, which states: When shooting a new scene, change the size of the image, or change the angle, or both.

• Image size can be changed by moving closer to or farther away from the subject, and this is accomplished through the LS, MS, CU, and the reestablishing shot.

• The general rule covers up jumpy action by distracting the audience's attention through the addition of something different to the new scene, and also enriches the motion picture by injecting visual variety.

• Angle changes provide infinite ways of applying the general rule.

• Image size can also be changed by the use of lenses of different focal length, like the long, the wide-angle and zoom lenses. The zoom combines the functions of the normal, long, and wide-angle lenses. However, be careful about the effect of these lenses in distorting perspective.

• Avoid using the zoom lens indiscriminately and to excess.

• Useful and convenient though these lenses may be, there are few movie story situations encountered by the beginning filmmaker that cannot be covered with an ordinary lens.

CHAPTER 7

ANGLES

CHOICE OF ANGLES

The general rule approves of a change of angles with each new scene. Such a change assures smooth continuity and variety. But just how good, how effective that change will be, is up to the cameraman.

Angles are an important part of his shooting style. The choice of angles can be as critical to his work as an author's choice of words. Angles can create drama, excitement, suspense. A story can be told more concisely in one good angle shot than in several scenes whose angles are uninspired.

Some of Hollywood's most brilliant cinematographers have made their reputations through a resourceful use of angles. They have rejuvenated subjects that were shot a thousand times before, removing all triteness with one dramatic, unexpected angle.

The usual angle of vision is the straight, normal, eye-level angle. As the eye moves along in its daily operations, this angle is constantly, infinitely varied by high angles looking down on some subject, low angles looking up, and side angles. There is an endless shifting and combination of these angles as we walk down the street, buy a paper, board a bus, gaze up at our office building as we enter, glance down at our desk to see what mail has come. And as with the human eye, there are endless variations for the resourceful cameraman.

THE FLAT ANGLE

There is one type of angle, however, that is commonplace and uninspired. Despite its name, it is really no angle at all. It is shot with the plane of the camera parallel to the plane of the subject. So observed, the subject cannot be seen "in the round"; it lacks depth, becomes flat and two-dimensional.

Flat Angle

Oblique Angle

Take a look at the shots of the early American locomotive above. The one on the left was made from a flat angle; it looks as static as it is. The shot on the right was made from an oblique angle with the camera viewfinder taking in the front of the locomotive as well as its side. The subject immediately gains depth and variety; it *looks* dynamic, as though the old coal burner is ready to roar down the rails.

The flat angle is particularly to be guarded against in *stationary* subjects like a house or anything motionless. However, it becomes a useful tool when shooting subjects moving toward the camera head-on, such as a child running right at you, since it carries constant interest because of the motion. Although the shot is flat, the angle of vision is constantly changing, and change makes for variety.

THE POWER OF ANGLES

Camera angles can control an audience's attention and reactions to a remarkable degree. They can emphasize *what* you want your audience to see and *how* you want them to see it.

Shrewd "angling" of the camera will enable you to control background and foreground and eliminate any feature that distracts from the subject.

High angles (in which the camera looks down) ordinarily give the illusion of reducing the height of a subject and slowing down its motion; *low angles* (in which the camera looks up) exaggerate height, and seem to speed up subject motion when comparatively near the camera.

Try shooting one of the classic subjects in the home movie library—Junior taking a ride on a pony. Get yourself some elevation like the upper story of a building and take some footage of Junior ambling along. Then return to the ground and drop to one knee with your camera as he passes by. When you screen your footage you will see how angles have affected your subject's size and speed of movement. For one thing, your high angle creates a certain feeling of "superiority" in the audience. It looks *down* on Junior. His size is foreshortened; he appears earthbound; his action seems insignificant, but when the next shot shows Junior from a low angle, looking *up* at him, audience psychology is reversed. Junior gains stature; he commands attention; there are drama and excitement in his actions.

A low angle also relieves the drabness of a flat angle shot at eye level. A *low oblique* angle adds greatly to the drama of the shot.

High Angle

Low Angle

Side angles are valuable for giving depth and perspective to people or objects. They help the audience see the subject in the round. Cleverly used, side angles can make a subject appear thinner or chubbier, as the cameraman desires.

While head-on angles give the illusion of reducing speed, side angles— especially the right angle—appear to increase speed. Suppose you shot a sequence of the last lap of a horse race from a position at the finish line. If you make a long shot as the leading horses start down the home stretch, your head-on angle will make their movements seem slow compared to the flashing speed of a right-angle shot as they dart past your camera at the finish line. But don't bet any money on a horse shot from a low side angle. That exaggerated speed is just a powerful illusion.[22]

ANGLES AND PSYCHOLOGY

More is involved in the use of angles than merely audience's concepts of movement and distance. We have noted how a high or low angle changes audience psychology. A definite emotional and mental attitude can be evoked by taking advantage of the audience's instinctive urge to identify itself with the camera viewpoint.

Suppose you are shooting sequences of mother with her child in a carriage. If your shots in the first sequence are from a normal eye-level angle, the audience is inclined to feel that it is bystander, a spectator.

But if, in your next sequence, you shoot baby using a high angle from the spot where mother is standing—from mother's viewpoint, as it were—the audience will unconsciously identify itself with her. And if you take a third sequence shooting mother from baby's position in the carriage, with a low angle, your audience will associate itself with baby, and look at things from her point of view.

DON'T BE "ANGLE CRAZY"!

So stimulating and rewarding are angle shots that the cameraman may be tempted to let his enthusiasm gallop away with his judgment. Being "angle crazy" is almost as bad as being "pan or zoom happy." Angles, like any any other aspect of motion-picture technique, are only a means to an end—the objective of good continuity. If they are indulged in for their own sake, they become trick shots, nothing more.

Trick angles might be justified if you were shooting a circus movie, where the freak, the grotesque, and the exaggerated are the order of the day. But the everyday world *is* not a circus world, and ordinary happenings are not usually observed from bizarre angles.

An angle so unusual that the audience's concentration is interrupted by the thought "that's a wild shot!" is a poor one because you have interfered with your audience's attention to the main action.

On the other hand, if an unusual angle points up to action and strengthens the audience's concentration, it is a good angle, for then the audience is *not* conscious of the angle *as such* and its attention is not distracted from the action.

Suppose two men are sitting at a table playing cards. A low-angle shot of the host, taken from the level of his calf looking up at him, would be an unusual angle all right, but nothing would be gained by it except the impression that the cameraman had tried something in the way of a trick. The main action still is *the card-playing.*

If the host's dog comes along, however, and rubs against his leg, disturbing him, a low-angle shot from the dog's level would be ideal to tell the story of how the host is distracted and looks down at the animal. The main action is now provided *by the dog* and the low angle becomes the most effective one. It is an integral part of the picture.

Smoothness, may we say again, is one of the outstanding qualities of good continuity. A smooth movie style must avoid angles that irritate and call attention to themselves, just as a smooth writing style must avoid similes or metaphors that are pretentious or too odd.

A good angle, in short, is one that calls attention to the action—not to itself.

SUMMARY

A cameraman's choice of angles is an important part of his style.

• A change of angles between shots not only enables application of the general rule; it also brings drama and excitement to the action.

• The human eye-level angle is constantly varied by high, low, and side angles.

• The so-called "flat angle" lacks interest and should be avoided except when the subject is moving head-on toward the camera, in which case the motion itself creates the interest.

• Angles can mold an audience's concept of the size and speed of movement of the subject on-screen. They can also influence the audience's psychological attitude toward the subject.

• Don't be "angle crazy." Avoid excessive use of unusual angles, which contribute to a picture only if they serve to clarify it and further the action.

• A good angle is one that calls attention to the action, not to itself.

CHAPTER 8

PANNING

CAUTION! PANNING AHEAD!

We come now to the subject of *panning,* which we have previously (in connection with its usefulness in the reestablishing shot) mentioned as a troublesome kind of shot. The problem is that panning is an exciting, dynamic kind of shot but is often abused. It can enrich pictorial continuity but it can also cause a lot of grief for the careless cameraman.

Before we go any further, let's understand the mechanics of a *pan.* In a pan shot, the camera is *rotated.* When a tripod or camera mount is used, the camera is rotated around its axis; when it is hand-held, the cameraman swings it around with his body as the axis of rotation.

The pan should not be confused with a *moving shot* in which the camera travels through space, such as on a moving car or train or hand-held by a walking cameraman.

Although the camera moves slightly in a hand-held pan, the cameraman remains in a fixed position; his body turns but he remains in place. You can, of course, have a *moving pan shot,* in which the cameraman pans while his body moves from one point to another as in a car on the road.

In the conventional pan, the camera is rotated along a horizontal plane. There are times when you will want to rotate the camera vertically, up or down. Strictly speaking, these vertical camera moves should be referred—for instant clarity—as "tilt up" or "tilt down," but you will find that "pan up" or "pan down" is also used.[23]

Indiscriminate panning, like zooming, is one of the most common faults of the beginner cameraman. It arises from the utterly mistaken fancy that a motion picture is most truly *moving* when the camera itself is in motion; that if the ball in a tennis game is jumping back and forth across the net, the camera must jump too.

This fallacy has caused many horrible mistakes to be committed in the name of panning. Audiences pay for them in eyesore and irritation. You may have a fine time making your pan, but if it bothers your audience, your reputation as a cameraman is worthless.

Like drinking for some people, panning is best when done least. However, a pan does have its uses in providing variety and excitement, and there are certain times when it is just about compulsory. That phase "certain times" is most important. You must learn the right occasion for the pan—and the right way of doing it. So, if you must gratify that over-powering temptation to pan, hold back until you learn the principles of *when* and *how*.

THE "WHEN" OF PANNING

Panning is rightly used to *follow action*.[24] It is a natural type of shot for filming a horse race or catching Junior as he pedals down the sidewalk on his tricycle. These sequences could be covered—in most cases—by pulling back to a long shot instead of by panning. But the shots—especially that of the galloping ponies—would be less effective on-screen. And if you wanted a closeup while your subject was in motion you would naturally pan. Following action is the big reason for panning.

In shooting a *static scene*, where there is no movement in or out of the frame, panning is *only rarely* justified. There are certain specialized cases. Scenic panning, for instance, can be excused when the subject is of such epic dimensions—New York harbor or the Grand Canyon—that only the full sweep of the pan can do it justice.[25]

Panning would be appropriate to show the intricate industrial relationship of the parts of an assembly line in an industrial plant, but in such a case moving objects or workers would probably give you a chance to pan by following action—always more desirable than panning a static subject.

If, also, you want to give dramatic emphasis to the height of a tall building or other vertical structure, you can tilt up slowly from ground level to the top. Take note that it is the *length* of the shot, not the angle, that creates the dramatic emphasis.

When you are shooting scenery from a moving train or boat, panning is quite automatic, since you yourself are moving. In case you want to swing your camera in a true pan, you should do so from forward (that is, from the direction of travel) back, so that your pan moves in the same direction in which the scenery appears to be traveling. Also, panning *against* your movement may produce a blurring effect.

It may be readily seen from these specialized cases where panning a static scene is justified, that the cameraman has a continuity idea in mind. Panning a static scene should never be done just because you don't want to back off far enough to cover the whole scene in one or more long shots.

THE "HOW" OF PANNING

No pan, no matter how justifiable or effective in theory, is any good if badly done. Far better than a bad pan is no pan at all, since a jerky, wavering, wildly racing shot will kill all interest in your picture.

The physical elements of a good pan are steadiness, evenness, slowness. They must be carefully studied and practiced, especially when shooting static objects where the lack of these qualities becomes distressingly noticeable. A correctly used tripod will ensure these qualities. For the many pans that you may have to make with your camera held only in your hands, a good stance is all-important.

Camera Pressed against Forehead or Cheeks and Held Firmly

Swing from Head and Shoulders Down through Hips and Ankles

Arms Close to Body, Elbows against Sides

Feet Planted Firmly on Ground, Pointed in Direction of Where Pan is to End

The stance for making a hand-held pan is identical with the stance for making any hand-held shot. Get a solid base, your feet firmly planted on the ground, spread apart, with your weight slightly forward. Either foot may be advanced for comfort. Ideally, your feet should be placed so as to point in the direction the pan is expected to end.

Next, give the camera triangular support by holding your arms close to your body, digging your elbows into your stomach, and pressing the camera against your forehead or cheek. Not every camera permits the use of *both* arms and elbows this way—but one is always better than none.

Lightweight video cameras are more easily hand-held but they are also more sensitive to any shakiness in your grip and transfer it to your pan. Steadiness, steadiness!

When panning, swing not just from your head and shoulders, but all the way down, from hips and ankles. If a tripod is used, you must maintain a firm grip on the camera and your body should swivel as you follow the pan.

Evenness and *slowness* are not always possible when following *action* with a pan. In such shots as a bucking bronco at a rodeo, or the antics of the family dog as he plays with a ball, you have to pan fast or slow, change your rate of speed according to the behavior of your moving subject. Your audience will not be upset, because its attention is focused on the action and it has no chance to think of anything else. There is, however, *no* excuse for lack of *steadiness* in a pan, regardless of action or the absence of it. Steadiness is a "must" quality in panning. If you can't make a steady pan, don't pan, *don't!*

A pan must be *level* throughout, with neither a sideways nor an up-or-down movement at any point in the film, otherwise your audience will find itself looking cockeyed at the subject matter. You *may* have to pan—or tilt up—with your camera if you follow an airplane taking off; but here the action accounts for the tilt and the audience is not made conscious of any bad camera handling on your part. It helps to find a level line like the horizon or a building roof in your frame and keep your frame line parallel with it.

An *even, constant rate* of panning is most important for smoothness. Irregularities in the rate of panning will cause your picture to move across the screen in jerks and will immediately distract the audience from the action to the failings of the cameraman. Even if, when following action, you cannot maintain a constant rate of movement, you *can* speed it up or slow it down *smoothly.* If the action—such as the playful dog—stops momentarily, then you stop panning momentarily; but there is no excuse for lack of smoothness when the subject is in motion. Like steadiness, smoothness is a "must" quality in the pan. Make your pans smooth![26]

Panning a static scene must be done *slowly.* Otherwise, no matter how steady or smooth your pan is, the result will be disastrous. If your subject is not in motion and you pan it quickly, it will be blurred. Of all the mechanical errors in panning, a very fast pan, with resultant blurring of the scene, is the most common. By comparison, an over-slow pan is a rarity, indeed. Don't trust the judgment of your eye on the speed of a pan. No matter how slow you judge it to be, it will *invariably* appear faster on the screen. So when you get set to make your pan at the slowest speed you consider desirable, just leap over backward and deliberately make it even slower.

Furthermore, the apparent speed of the pan is very definitely affected by the distance between the camera and the subject. If possible, avoid panning a *moving* subject when it is too close to the camera, for only the most precise camera handling will keep the picture from flashing by on the screen. For the same reason, don't pan with a telephoto lens unless *following action,* for even the slowest speed will cause your scene to race by in a blur.

The physical qualities of a good pan are plainly not something to be picked up in a moment. Practice is essential. A useful habit to get into is to "dry run" your pan—to rehearse, without pressing the button, the movement your camera will make in the air. Figure how your pan *will end,* and adjust the preceding motion to that.

OTHER FACTORS

There are other factors which improve a well-made pan. The human eye usually looks at a scene from left to right, or from the bottom up. Pan and tilt that way, when the action allows. Of course, following action such as kids romping in a playground will cause you to switch direction. But when your audience is absorbed in the action, it will not be distracted by this fact.[27]

By all means avoid "whitewashing" a static scene—waving your camera back and forth as though you were using a paint-brush.

It is desirable when panning action to precede the actual pan with a brief, non-pan shot of the subject; and to follow up the pan immediately with a similar shot ot the last scene, before stopping the camera. Thus if Betty runs after a ball, try to open the shooting with a steady, non-pan shot as she starts her sprint; pan her over to where she retrieves the ball; and end the sequence with another non-pan shot of her. These "before-and-after" non-pan shots give your audience a chance to see what is going on *before* the camera moves, and to orient itself again to the scene that *follows* the completion of the pan.

It is jarring to the audience to be switched abruptly from a still to an action pan or from an action pan to a still scene. But of the two faults, the latter is much worse and less excusable. Many times it is impossible to begin an action pan with a non-pan shot. This especially holds true when the action is uncontrolled—in a horse race or track meet, for instance, where your subjects are in high speed all the time. It is difficult to find an excuse, however, for not holding your camera motionless at the end of the pan. Either your subject will come to rest, or you can simply stop the pan and allow the action *to move out of the frame* while you hold your camera immobile. It is extremely upsetting to the audience to see something that is in full motion on the screen abruptly cut off in mid-action. Give action a clean exit, so that it disappears logically.

Even if an obstruction, such as a football spectator jumping up and down while you're panning a touchdown run, momentarily cuts off your view, always follow through on your action; keep right on panning so that you will pick up the action again beyond the obstruction and hold it until it moves out of the frame.

This point is so important that we repeat: *Avoid cutting from the middle of an action pan to a still scene.* Let your action move out of the frame. You've surely seen many a good newsreel sequence of a horse race where the cameraman (stationed at the finish line) picked up the ponies in motion at the far end of the straightaway, panned them until they moved up opposite to him, held the camera steady as they crossed the finish line then stopped it only *after* they had moved out of the frame.

When you get down to editing your footage, you will thank yourself profusely for having followed through with your camera and allowed the action to move cleanly out of the frame.

PLAN YOUR PANS

As you pan action closer to you, it will naturally become larger, thus commanding more of your audience's attention. As you pan action away from you, it grows smaller, and there is an inevitable—if relatively slight—drop in audience interest. Therefore, try to plan your pans so that they reach their climax when the action fills the screen. Conversely, try to avoid beginning a pan at a ninety-degree angle to your subject. Start it from a narrow, acute angle.

A pan has "buildup" quality. It should gain in interest as it moves along and its conclusion should be its high point, its peak of action and excitement. Otherwise your audience will be let down. A racing pan is more exciting if it picks up the horses at the beginning of the home stretch and reaches its climax as they cross the finish line, than if it starts with the finish of the race and follows through on the horses as they slow down and stop. The point is that the finish line is the visual climax of the pan. However, it is perfectly logical to continue panning the winning horse to show his jockey slowing him to a halt. That completes the action. It also gives the audience a chance to wind down after the exciting climax.

One criminal perversion of the pan is to use it just to cover a lot of ground while shifting from one point of interest to another—a mistake very often made in a scenic pan. Don't be led astray by the fallacy that this is the way the human eye operates when it looks from one thing to another. The eye does not truly pan—it *jumps* from one scene to another, skipping whatever is uninteresting during the jump. While it is in motion, it sees nothing it doesn't want to see. Let your glance shift from one corner to another of a strange room and try to remember just what you have seen inbetween!

CAUTION AGAIN!

We have granted the good points, the special usefulness of the pan. We endorse it with reluctance because, as this chapter has made plain, a well-made, well-thought-out pan is no easy matter. We reiterate: Better no pan at all than a bad pan. Remember, no picture ever suffered from a lack of pans as long as the action could be covered otherwise. And there are mighty few instances where the action could *not* be covered otherwise.

Have pity on your audience—approach the pan with caution and respect. Use it sparingly—no matter how well you do it. Of course, telling a beginner cameraman to go easy on panning is about as effective as telling a Little Leaguer to hold back on trying to knock the ball out of the park the first time he comes up to bat. If you are that beginner, we hope you'll get the urge to pan just for the kick of panning out of your system—fast!

SUMMARY

Indiscriminate panning is one of the most common faults of the beginner cameraman.

- Panning has its uses but the cameraman should learn *when* and *how*.
- The *when* of panning applies to following action or to shooting certain static scenes where the pan can make clearer either size or the relationship of parts.
- The *how* of panning requires steadiness of stance, keeping the camera level and moving it smoothly and evenly. When the scene is static, the pan *must* be made slowly.
- Avoid "whitewashing" a static scene.
- Hold the camera steady for a moment before beginning and after ending a pan. If the action is not to be followed through, let it go cleanly out of the frame before stopping the camera.
- Avoid cutting from the middle of an action pan to a still scene.
- The end of the pan is the climax of subject movement. It should also be the climax of interest. If possible, shoot the pan from the position where it will reach its climax. Make the beginning from an acute angle and pan through until the action fills the frame.
- Do not pan merely to avoid moving back far enough to get all the subject in the frame with a single long shot.
- A pan is rarely indispensable to a picture and a bad pan is much worse than no pan at all.
- Avoid panning whenever possible unless following action.

CHAPTER 9

MOVING SHOTS

DOLLYING IN AND OUT

Up to now we have stressed the importance of keeping the camera as steady and stationary as possible. But frequently we can tell a motion picture story more effectively by using *moving shots.* These are shots in which the camera is shooting *while it is in motion.*

As we mentioned in the chapter on the simple sequence in which Mr. Producer was our subject, one method of going from a long shot to a closeup was by using a mobile camera platform known as a "dolly."

Dollying in to your subject and *dollying out or back* gives you a complete sequence without breaking it up into separate LS, MS and CU. When smoothly done, a dolly shot can stimulate audience interest as it moves in to a closeup. If we started out with an MS of mother holding a birthday cake and dollied in on the cake slowly to a CU, the gradual enlargement of the cake—its seeming to "grow" till it is full screen—would steadily build up audience interest.

Or suppose you want to make a long closeup of mother kissing baby. The heads of both your subjects already fill the frame. To keep the lengthy shot from being tedious, you want to move your camera a bit. This does not mean you must dolly in; you are already on a closeup! But you can dolly *sideways*—slowly—so that you gradually change the angle even to the point of moving the camera behind mother for an over-the-shoulder shot of baby's face. This gradual change of angle gives the shot visual variety; its slow movement fits the gentle mood of the action. But be sure the dolly is smooth.

THE TRUCKING SHOT

Another type of moving shot is the *trucking shot,* in which the camera moves *along with* the subject, usually maintaining approximately the same image size as it follows the action. An example is a steadily maintained close shot of a child reacting to the wonders it sees as her mother wheels her carriage down the street.[28]

Another example of a trucking shot is to follow a speeding automobile from another car going just as fast.

DO IT YOURSELF—IMPROVISE!

Professional motion picture and television companies make their moving shots with specially designed equipment. Very often, it is elaborate to the point where the dolly is mounted on tracks, not only in the studio, but outdoors, on location. High-angle moving shots are made from mobile cranes or similar equipment, or from trucks or cars with a camera platform rigged on the roof.

But you don't have to go Hollywood to do moving shots. Any cameraman can improvise a satisfactory dolly. Borrow a ride in Junior's wagon, or have your neighbor drive you down the street while you shoot from the car window. Any moving vehicle can serve as a mobile camera platform. Your body too! TV news cameramen often must depend on so-called walking shots when they want to follow action or dolly in or out.

The trick, of course, is to bring off a smooth, steady walking shot. Obviously, you can't use a tripod, so it's important to use the correct method of making a hand-held shot described in the chapter on panning. Make it a matter of automatic habit by practising, and when the subject allows, rehearse your shot with a dry run.

You must keep checking focus as you dolly in or out. That's so critical that in Hollywood, *follow focus* is the job of the assistant cameraman.

Again, we must bear down with a word of caution: your moving shots will be effective *only* as long as the audience is not made aware of the method by which they were obtained. That is why Hollywood goes to such great trouble and expense to do its moving shots in an unobtrusive manner.

The moment your audience is distracted from the story by poor technique, such as unsteadiness, fuzzy focus or other faults, your moving shot joins the class of the bad pan and must be condemned as worse than no moving shot at all.

THE VERSATILE ZOOM LENS

The zoom lens produces a similar effect to the dolly in or dolly out and has advantages in several respects. The rate of movement of the zoom lens is variable—from very slow to very fast—whereas the dolly must move relatively slowly to maintain the same degree of steadiness. Nor do you have to check focus as you zoom. A very fast zoom in from LS to CU—sometimes called an "explosion" shot—can produce a very dramatic effect.[29]

A unique advantage of the zoom lens is that it can instantaneously leap a space barrier. Suppose you are shooting a football game from the stands.

Without moving your camera, you can go from a wide-angle shot taking in both teams to a closeup of the man carrying the ball, while keeping the action centered in the frame and in focus throughout!

A zoom shot can be equally effective at close quarters. As a matter of fact, the ingenious cameraman can simulate a short zoom with just a wide-angle lens—preferably an extreme wide-angle, such as 10mm lens on a 16mm camera.

Suppose you are shooting a sequence about signing an important document—a contract with Mr. Producer. You want to start with an over-the-shoulder shot as he begins to sign, then zoom into a CU of the contrast as he finishes.

Take a firm stance with your feet, *because you will not move them,* then lean back as far as you comfortably can, framing Mr. Producer in the left-hand side of the frame and the contrast in the right background. As he starts to sign, bring the upper part of your body forward, shooting as you move, until you fill the screen with the contract.

The camera will move just a few feet—perhaps only two and a half from wide shot to CU—but the extreme wide-angle lens will provide a zoom-like change of image size.[30]

Once you master this improvised zoom shot—and it takes only a little practice—you will find it has versatile uses. Try it for catching facial expressions of spontaneous reaction. For example, move in from a medium close shot of an expectant father to a full closeup when the nurse tells him "it's a boy."

A warning—since you must close your lens diaphragm down far enough to get proper depth of field for this shot, make sure your light source has sufficient brightness to allow it.

PLEASE DO NOT ABUSE!

Because the zoom shot is so spectacular and the zoom lens so easy to operate, it is wildly abused through excessive use as previously mentioned. This abuse is probably the most common fault of the student cameraman and, too often, of many professionals as well, particularly those who work in documentaries and television news.[31]

In the case of the beginner, this abuse may be condoned as the self-indulgence of the amateur who is just learning about the remarkable visual potential of his equipment by playing around with it. There is really no excuse for the professional who should know better than to be "zoom happy" or—when there is no space barrier—is simply too lazy to walk a short distance so that he can shoot a closer angle with an ordinary lens.[32]

Like so many eye-catching shots, the tremendous pictorial and dramatic impact of a zoom is quickly frittered away by overuse: The spectacular becomes monotonous through pointless repetition. Just as bad, it becomes an irritant to the audience. The sensational speed with which a scene is rushed in close to the viewer's eye produces a visual shock. When zooms follow one another in rapid succession, they cause eyestrain *and* mental discomfort. Too many zooms are made much too fast, anyway—especially when the action is relatively static.

Also, when you cover too much of the action with zoom shots, you make it difficult to edit them effectively. Just try cutting into the middle of a zoom! This is especially hazardous when you are simultaneously recording live sound— a speech or on an interview. Don't forget that the film or tape editor may be you! So please, as aforementioned, use zoom shots carefully—and with restraint.

These problems in using the zoom lens can be avoided by the disciplined cameraman who knows—and practices—his craft. There are, however, some built-in disadvantages to the zoom which make the dolly-in a superior moving shot in situations where normal camera movement is called for. A zoom-in distorts perspective; a dolly-in does not. Another disadvantage is that the angle of view narrows with a zoom-in; it remains the same in a dolly-in with an ordinary lens.[33]

SUMMARY

A motion picture story can often be told more effectively by means of *moving shots,* in which the camera itself is in motion.

• A familiar type of moving shot is the dolly-in or dolly-out, in which the camera moves toward or away from the subject. Another is the trucking shot, in which the camera moves along with the subject, usually maintaining the same image size.

• A mobile camera platform for moving shots can be improvised by using any available moving vehicle—or even the cameraman's own body.

• The zoom lens can produce a similar effect as the dolly-in or -out without moving the camera. Avoid the temptation—and the editing problems—of using it to excess.

CHAPTER 10

DIRECTIONAL CONTINUITY

CONSTANT SCREEN DIRECTION

The screen has unlimited power of illusion. But "illusion" is not far removed in sound or spelling from "confusion," and the unwary cameraman will often find his camera prankishly playing tricks on his audience against his best wishes and intentions.

We have said before and resoundingly say again that the cameraman must enable his audience to see the action on-screen the way he sees it in reality. He must continuously take into account the fact that what he sees *directly* with the freedom and mobility of his eyes, is seen at second hand by the audience on a screen of rigid dimensions. The eye can pick and choose, but the screen *imposes* its story on the audience.

This is the danger of screen illusion. It can make confusing little, simple acts that are never misconstrued by the human eye when it sees them in real life.

Take the matter of movement. You come across a parade on an avenue in your home town, and the marchers move across your vision from *left* to *right*. You cross the street and look back: the paraders march now from *right* to *left*. This is perfectly understandable to you, so understandable that you never stop to think consciously of it. Your mind has automatically taken into account the shift in your position to a reverse angle of view, from which things naturally take the opposite aspect; you are fully aware that the parade is still moving in the same forward direction.

But if you were to make a motion picture of that parade, first from one side of the street, and then from the other, the marchers would appear to be moving in exactly opposite directions on the street; the audience could not help being somewhat bewildered, lacking an explanation on the screen for the change.

The first answer to the problem presented by a confusing position change is: Avoid it. Do so by maintaining *constant screen direction*. If you shoot a se-

CHANGE OF SCREEN DIRECTION
Wherein the Action Explains the Change

Top to Bottom

Establishing Shot	*Medium Shot*
Medium Shot	*Reestablishing Shot*
Closeup	

quence of the marchers, keep them moving in the same direction in all shots. If they move initially from left to right, keep all shots left to right; if they start from right to left, keep all shots right to left. Try to avoid direction changes between shots.

Sometimes your action will logically change screen direction. No problem as long as the sequence of shots makes the reason clear. As an example take as your subject mother and little sister Betty in the park playing with a ball. You want to show a sequence showing Betty going after the ball, picking it up and returning to mother with it. Change of direction is obviously going to be involved, but you have no problem as long as you make sure your camera tells the whole story. You shoot a LS showing the two subjects and the start of the action, move in for a MS of Betty going after the ball, follow that with a CU cut-in of her hand grasping the ball, then move back to a MS showing her turning with the ball now in her hand, and finish the sequence with a LS of her coming back to Mother in the opposite direction. The CU cut-in and the following MS showing the turn are your key shots here; they reconcile the audience to the direction change; they are easy to make yet the lack of them would make the sequence confusing. The success of directional continuity depends very often on not neglecting elementary shots.

MASKING DIRECTION CHANGES

Trouble may arise, however, in sequences where the action moves only one way but where, in order to photograph the story properly, you cannot avoid shots with different screen directions.

It may happen in the case of the parade that colorful backgrounds on *both* sides of the street compel you to shoot from either side, with resultant changes in screen direction of the marchers. Again, on a boat trip down a river, your picture might show departure from a river town on one side and arrival at a river town on the *other* side. En route, you might wish to shoot interesting buildings or scenery on *either bank* or boats passing on *either side* of you.

Obviously, switching your shots back and forth from one side to the other would result in many changes of screen direction, resulting in confusion.

Confusion would be possible, but *not* inevitable. That same power of screen illusion which creates all this directional trouble now comes to the rescue. It can be applied to avoid confusion in several ways, but there is one technique that is far and away the best because it is most effective and most easily and universally used. That is *distraction.*

THE TECHNIQUE OF DISTRACTION

Using the versatile cinema tools of cut-in and cut-away, distraction exploits the continuity truism mentioned previously: An audience, always looking ahead to what is coming on the screen, rarely keeps in mind *more than one scene prior to the one it is looking at.*

The distraction technique separates scenes of a sequence which have conflicting screen directions by an intermediate shot—or shots (it is always better to have two or more instead of just one) in which there is no cross-screen direction of movement.

If cut-ins are used, the shots can be head-ons, tail-aways, or both. The parade will serve as an example. You are shooting the procession as it passes from left to right when you notice you are on the same side of the street as the reviewing stand. Since your climactic scene is to be the marchers passing in front of this most important background, you must cross the street to shoot it. But a shot from that side would show the marchers from right to left. So, before changing over, you take a cut-in shot in which the screen direction is neutral.

You step into the gap *between* two groups of marchers and shoot either the first group from the rear as it moves *away* from the camera, or the second group from the front as it moves *toward* the camera. In these shots the marchers do not have cross-screen direction; your audience ceases to be conscious of any such direction; and the climactic shot may therefore be taken without confusion from the other side of the street and show a right-left direction.

Cut-aways, similarly used, produce the same distraction even more effectively, because their subject, although related to the main action, *is completely separate from it.*

In the case of the parade, cut-aways may consist of spectators, of confetti raining down from the buildings, of flags flying along the line of march. Such shots take your audience eye completely away from the parade and the direction in which it is moving. If you then switch back to the parade from a different side of the street, your audience is not confused because it will have forgotten the original screen direction.

The boat-trip example has plenty of opportunities for cutaway distraction shots in closeups of passengers, of sailors, of boat-details like pennants flying, hawsers being hauled in and carefully piled, furrows cut in the water by the ship's prow.

To avoid a troublesome misconception in the reader's mind, we wish to bring out here an important point that is properly a function of *editing.*

A cameraman shooting distraction shots on film may find it more convenient to shoot them out of order just like any inserts, examples—the spectators or flags at the parade before it begins or, similarly, some of the details aboard ship at the beginning or end of the trip. The cameraman knows that during editing, these distraction shots can be smoothly inserted in the action where they can do their job of masking changes in screen direction. The end product—*what the audience sees on the screen*—is the important thing.

However, when the distraction shots are on videotape, we run into the same problem of clean editing we described for inserts unless the editor has electronic editing equipment. In such a case, the cameraman is wise to shoot his distraction shots in the precise continuity order in which they are meant to be seen by the audience.[34]

OTHER METHODS

The resources of screen illusion can be applied in specialized cases to *deceiving* an audience into accepting a reversal of screen direction.

An example is the boat trip down the river where you constantly have to switch the camera from one bank to the other. Ask some lens struck spectator (whom you're sure to find in any situation!) to pose as an actor for you. Frame him in the foreground as he looks over the rail at the river bank which is moving by from *left* to *right.*

Now ask your actor to turn his head so that his gaze shifts to the other side. Shoot his action with the camera. That simple action of turning his head has *suggested* a change of direction. You can now shoot the other bank of the river from *right* to *left* and your audience will accept the reversal contentedly.

Still another way of keeping your audience satisfied about screen direction is to keep the same landmark, symbol, or object in the background in successive shots with different screen directions, so that its position in regard to the action keeps the direction of movement clear.

To illustrate: You are shooting a sequence of the lady of the house clipping roses from a bush on the front lawn. Your neighbor, Mr. Montgomery, walks by from *right* to *left.* He is dressed carefully, his step is brisk, he is very, very definitely *going somewhere.*

When he sees your wife, however, he stops for a moment to say hello and to admire the roses. On the spur of the moment you decide to "shoot him into the story." Your establishing shot was from out in the street, with the rosebush *behind.* Mr. Montgomery. It is to his right, in the direction from which he has come.

You close in for MS's and CU's, but to get a fresh angle and to fill up your background as much as possible with that handsome rosebush, you change to a shooting position on the lawn, on the other side of Mr. Montgomery. The rosebush is now on his left in the background.

Mr. Montgomery is in very much of a hurry, unfortunately, and waits only until you finish your MS before he rushes off. As he leaves, you manage to pan him away and let him walk out of the frame, but now his screen direction is from *left* to *right.* There has been no time for distraction cut-ins, no time to switch back to your original angle from the street.

But the rosebush is *still behind him.* He has had his back to it consistently while he spoke to your wife, and the audience will know that he has not changed but his moving in one constant direction all the time—*away* from the rosebush.

The use of this method of masking direction changes is limited, of course, to scenes where a recognizable object is consistently seen and where the position of that object relative to the action helps keep direction clear.

A sensitivity to screen direction is one of the refinements of good continuity. It helps differentiate the knowledgeable cameraman from the amateurish button-pusher.[35]

DIRECTIONAL CONTINUITY IN TRAVEL SEQUENCES

Whenever a considerable amount of travel is being recorded on film or videotape, directional continuity becomes more important than ever. This is not only because you must avoid confusing your audience about *which way you are going,* but also because you have to convince it that *you are getting there.*

If you shoot your travelogue of a vacation trip to New York City from somewhere out West, the same screen direction should be maintained regardless of the time interval between shots.

Let's say you're shooting your arrival at, and departure from, a picturesque lodge where you stay overnight en route. You shoot the car as your wife drives it up to the lodge entrance from left to right. Next morning, when you wife drives off, make sure that she goes out of the frame *to the right.* If she drives off to the left—in the opposite direction—the audience will feel that you are going back to where you came from. The actual time interval between shots was many hours; on screen it is no more than a split second. That is how continuity gremlins make illusion work the wrong way.

So great is the power of movie suggestion that sometimes you must "cheat" on the truth about screen direction. In this particular example, to get to the main highway again and resume your trip, you may actually have to retrace your entrance and drive off *to the left.* But if you shot the truth, your audience would get the feeling that you were going back where you came from. Therefore, rather than go through all the trouble of explaining to your audience that you are *not* going back where you came from but are reversing direction *only momentarily* in order to get to the main highway before resuming *true direction,* it is much easier simply to shoot the car driving off *to the right,* stop the camera, turn your car around, and proceed merrily on your way.

Regard for the power of movie suggestion applies even to seemingly insignificant details of screen direction. If you shoot an insert of a map as your wife's hand traces your route on it, then follow with a shot of the car actually en route, be sure that the screen direction of both your wife's hand and the moving car are identical. Even in small things you should keep the illusion of constant screen direction unruffled.

CONTRASTING SCREEN DIRECTION

A reasonable inference from this discussion of changes in screen direction is that the whole matter is a nuisance, and that our preoccupation with it is wholly negative—to prevent audience confusion.

Once again, however, we find a continuity cloud that has a silver lining. Opposing screen directions *can* be used for positive purposes and do not present merely a negative problem. When different actors or actions are involved, they can create a very powerful feeling of suspense.

This effect is brought about by *contrasting* screen directions. Suppose you want to show two persons approaching each other. Their meeting will be the climax of the sequence. You want to build up to that climax, make the audience look forward to it, eagerly, expectantly.

Suppose you shoot a boy-meets-girl story in which our young friend Dean plays the juvenile lead. He is off on a blind date to play tennis with a girl named Trudy. You want to show Trudy and Dean approaching the tennis court separately. Both are anticipating the meeting, curious as to what the other looks like.

Familiar as this story is, you can easily build audience suspense with individual shots of each subject moving in opposite—contrasting—directions.

You shoot the sequence so that when it is put together, you first have an LS of Dean moving briskly from left to right; then an LS of Trudy approaching from right to left; next an MS of each, still maintaining contrasting screen direction, perhaps a little hesitant now, as they come closer and begin to have doubts about the blind date. If you wish, you can add separate closeups, thus heightening the suspense, with each subject still moving in contrasting directions. Finally, the two meet on the tennis court, obviously pleased with what the other looks like.

This shot is the climax of the sequence, paying off on the suspense we have built. So the angle is fairly close—a "full figure" or "two-shot." It is close enough to show their reaction to one another, yet clearly establishes the scene of their meeting as a tennis court.[36]

You can then move in to shoot a sequence of closer angles to build up their getting to know each other; then go on to show them playing tennis.

Although Dean and Trudy do not actually come together until the final scene, the contrasting screen directions of each give the audience a mounting anticipation of that coming-together. The alternating, increasingly close shots produce a feeling of excitement the audience will not experience if you shoot the entire sequence with both subjects on the screen at the same time.

This method of creating suspense is an old movie standby. It is used to create a feeling of fearful expectation in murder movies: the killer is shown stalking through the shadows from one direction in one scene, while in the next his unknowing victim is seen moving toward him from the opposite direction.

CONTRASTING SCREEN DIRECTION
To Create Suspense

LS (Dean, l to r.)

LS (Trudy, r. to l.)

MS (Dean, l. to r.)

MS (Trudy, r. to l.)

LS (Dean and Trudy, both)

MS (Dean and Trudy, both)

Every "horse opera" with its big climax of cowboys racing toward a meeting with a horde of Indians uses contrasting screen direction to build up the feeling of inevitable clash. With cowboys coming from left to right and Indians from right to left, the audience knows they are bound to meet. Excitement mounts accordingly.[37]

But note—and note carefully—that constant screen direction is maintained for each subject. The cowboys, whenever they appear on the screen, are *always* coming from left to right, and the Indians *always* from right to left. If this constancy were violated, if in one shot the Indians were shown moving from *left* to *right,* the audience impression would no longer be that they were running headlong toward a clash, but that they were running away, trying to escape from the cowboys!

And the confusion would become indescribable if directions were continually changed back and forth, both for the cowboys and the Indians. The audience could not be blamed for bewilderedly concluding that there were not two but a half-dozen different groups chasing and fleeing from each other all over the map.

So when using *contrasting* screen directions, make sure your individual actions maintain *constant* screen direction: The idea is to create suspense, not confusion.

The technique of cutting back and forth between related but separate actions is known as *cross-cutting.* It is used not only for contrasting screen direction, but also to tie together any concurrent actions which are related in theme but separate in space. If you had both cowboys and Indians riding in the same direction—one group chasing the other—continuity would be maintained through cross-cutting. Cross-cutting is a valuable technique for building up contrast, suspense or anticipation. You'll find it discussed further in the chapter on buildup.

CLEAN ENTRANCES AND EXITS

If you sat in the living room, closed your eyes for a moment, then opened them to find one of the family sitting in a hitherto vacant chair, you would certainly be startled. You would pop out the question: "How did you get there!" Your surprise would be involuntary even though a moment's reflection would tell you that the person had simply walked in.

A reaction of surprise would be just as inevitable if you closed your eyes again, and found on opening them once more that the occupant of the chair had vanished.

This shock of surprise affects a movie audience just as strongly when someone suddenly appears or disappears on the screen without the action's being accounted for. The cameraman may get away with popping people on and off the screen without explanation in trick photography whose purpose is deliberately to puzzle or dumbfound the audience. Pictorial continuity,

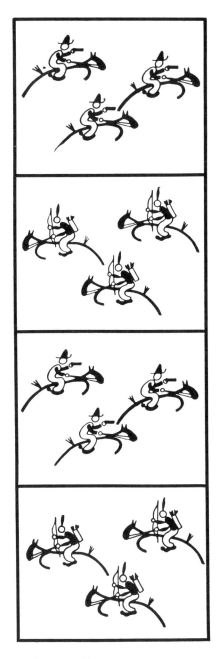

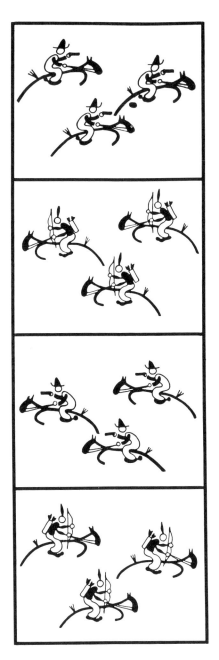

Left, Top to Bottom
  Constant Screen Direction

Right, Top to Bottom
  Confused Screen Direction

however, has just the opposite objective. In the normal movie, therefore, where clarity and cohesion are sought, a person on-screen should be shown *coming from somewhere* when he arrives on the scene and *going somewhere* when he departs from the scene.

The necessity for this seems childishly self-evident. It is *not* self-evident on the screen unless your actor makes clean screen exits and entrances.

Suppose you're hired to shoot a christening ceremony. One sequence shows the arrival of the godfather—the real kind, not the metaphorical figure in the famous gangster film. When he approaches to congratulate the beaming parents, let him make a clean entrance by coming in from outside the frame. The same goes for his departure from the scene. Let him walk completely out of the frame.

However—and this is a very important "however"—clean screen exits and entrances are imperative only when the presence of the actor concerned has not been registered in the establishing scene. When the christening scene opens, it shows the godfather already talking to the happy parents, his presence is established; the audience accepts him the same way it assumes that an actor it sees onstage in a play when the curtain rises has *already* made a logical entrance. Nor does the godfather have to make a clean entrance if you precede his MS or CU by an LS showing him in a group of guests being greeted by the parents; his presence is established by the group shot.

The same logic applies to clean exits. The godfather need not move individually out of the frame unless the very next shot shows the group without him. In that case you have to walk him out to explain his disappearance.

Whenever you shoot clean screen entrances and exits, make sure they are really *clean.* That is to say, if you want a clean entrance of the godfather, don't skimp on film by waiting for him to enter the frame of your viewfinder before starting to shoot. Let him come in cleanly from outside the frame. The same goes for his departure. When he takes leave of his hosts, don't stop shooting just as he approaches the other side of the frame.

Clean screen entrances and exits eliminate awkwardness and are always more dramatic.[38] The extent to which they affect smoothness of continuity was stressed in our discussion of panning, where we saw that there was a distressing jump in the action whenever it did not go cleanly out of the frame.

Actors in stage plays make clean-cut entrances and exits. Let your movie subjects do the same. They do not have to come through a door, window, or gate as a stage actor must, they need only come from beyond the screen boundary—and go out beyond it.

USING EFFECTS FOR CLEAN ENTRANCES AND EXITS

The idea of clean entrances and exits between sequences can be conveyed by various visual effects. These effects, whose names are very nearly self-explanatory although we will define them shortly, are *fade-ins, fade-outs, dissolves, blur pans, blur focus shots* and *wipes*. They announce the beginning or end of a sequence—the start of action or its conclu- sion—even though the subject does not physically enter or leave the scene.

All of these effects, except for complicated wipes, can be made with cameras available to the average cameraman. However, these so-called "in- camera" effects can't be changed once they are shot. If they turn out to be un- satisfactory, you would have to reshoot the scenes in which they are used. Thus, it is not the practice in professional productions to use in-camera effects. Any desired effects are added by means of an *optical printer,* which permits changes to be made, *after* the entire production has been filmed and com- pletely edited. They are, accordingly, known as *optical effects.* Here are some definitions:

In a *fade-in*, the scene gradually appears on a blank screen. The fade-in implies the idea of a clean entrance. *Fade-up* is the video term. To suggest the godfather's arrival, you could fade in on him as he stands in the church door- way being greeted by the parents. If you wanted to convey the *motion* of his ar- rival, you could fade in as he walks up the steps of the church.

A *fade-out* is the exact opposite of a fade-in. In a fade-out, the scene pro- gressively darkens until it becomes completely black. It clearly means the end of a sequence whether the action moves out of the frame or remains within it. The godfather's departure from the christening ceremony would be understood whether you faded out on him standing in the doorway saying goodbye to the parents or walking away down the church steps. The fade-out conveys finality even though he does not move out of the frame in a clean exit.

In a *dissolve,* the end of a scene blends into the beginning of the next scene so that for an instant, before the new scene entirely replaces the old one, the audience gets the effect of a double exposure. In essence, it is an overlap without matching action. The dissolve combines the ideas of clean exit and en- trance implied separately by the fade-out and fade-in. In the christening se- quence, a typical dissolve would blend from the godfather congratulating the parents at the church door to a scene of the same group taking their places at the baptismal font.

The *blur pan*[39] is made by rapidly panning the camera away from a scene just shot so rapidly that only a moving blur is recorded, then abruptly stopping the fast pan.The next scene in the story is shot in a normal way. Suppose you're doing a travel story and want to show the abrupt change between leav- ing a snowy northern city and entering a sunny one in the South. The se- quence would show a scene of you loading your car in a snowstorm and driving off, a blur pan, then a scene of you unloading the car in front of a hotel in a semi-tropical setting of bright sunshine and waving palm trees.[40]

The blur pan is a dynamic transition effect. You've seen it used in a news or documentary story about a politician who covers a lot of cities on a campaign tour. The blur pan graphically conveys the idea of the constant rush from one place to another.

By the way, don't make the mistake of thinking that the "blur" in *blur pan* means the scene goes out of focus. It does not. The blurred effect is created by the camera's speed of movement and by nothing else.

In a *blur focus shot*,[41] camera focus is made to blur until the subject becomes indistinct. Conversely, the next shot in the transition opens out of focus and is progressively made sharper until the subject—the same one as before or a different one—is clearly defined. This can be done in-camera by manipulating the focus adjustment; by movement, that is, by having the subject or the camera *move* toward the other without adjusting focus; or on the optical printer.[42]

Here are a couple of illustrations: We see a young man making a blind date with a girl over the phone. The cameraman goes out of focus on a closeup showing the young man's doubtful expression; then comes into focus on a closeup of a beautiful girl. The next shot shows her seated with the young man, who is smiling happily at his good luck.

About that traveling politician we can go out of focus on him speaking in one location and come into focus on him shaking hands in another. Or for that matter, we can blur out on him then blur into a shot of a rival politician, for the sake of contrast.

In a *wipe*, one scene replaces another so parts of both are onscreen simultaneously. There is no blending of scenes as in a dissolve. Instead, the scenes appear adjacent to one another with a clean-cut demarcation between them. Film wipes are made on the optical printer. They can be as simple as a *push-off* wipe in which a scene appears to be pushing off a preceding scene with a frame line separating the two; or assume much more complex form such as spiral wipes, iris wipes, burst wipes and so on. Video effects generators can create these wipes plus a variety of stunning visual effects. You see them constantly on TV news and sports broadcasts. They are comparable to film in quality and can be produced instantaneously.[43]

These visual effects are defined here because they can be used to imply clean entrances and exits; they serve primarily as time-space transition devices. Their purpose is to connect sequences smoothly. They should *not* be used as substitutes for clean entrances and exits when these are clearly called for by the script.

Nor should they be used loosely between shots of a sequence for the sake of the effect. It would make poor film sense—and it would be downright absurd—to fade in and out between shots of the godfather saying his farewells to members of the family and other guests, or fading out after his final farewell in the church doorway and fading in again to show him halfway down the steps as he leaves. The actual transition in time is just too short to justify the use of fades or any other mechanical effect.

The razzle-dazzle of these effects may tempt toward overuse, but they should be employed sparingly, when the needs of continuity override their obvious "trick" nature. More on their use will be found in the discussion of transition techniques in connection with "Juggling Time and Space." (See Chapter 12, Transitions in Time and Space).

SUMMARY

Changes of screen direction, unaccounted for by the action, confuse the audience.

• This confusion can be avoided by maintaining constant screen direction; that is, by keeping the action on-screen moving consistently from left to right or from right to left.

• When it is impossible to avoid reversals of screen direction unaccounted for by the action, changes of direction can be masked in several ways.

• One method, depending on *distraction,* draws the audience's attention away from the fact that a direction change has been made, by shooting the action in cut-ins, especially head-ons and tail-aways, so that no cross-screen direction of movement is apparent. Distraction can also be achieved through the use of cut-aways.

• Other methods of masking direction change include that of *deception,* which *suggests* change; and that of the use of the outstanding landmark or fixed background object.

• In travel movies, constant screen direction is necessary not only to make clear to the audience which way the subject is going, but also to convince it that the subject is getting there. Directional continuity must be maintained in *little* touches throughout the travel sequence.

• Opposing screen directions of different actors or actions create suspense by *contrast.*

• *Contrasting* screen direction is effective when directional continuity is maintained for each subject.

• Clean screen entrances and exits are important. Entering a scene, the subject should come cleanly into the frame from beyond it; leaving, he should go cleanly out of the frame. Audience surprise and confusion will result otherwise.

• Clean exits and entrances can be implied by visual effects such as fade-ins, fade-outs, dissolves, blur pans, blur focus shots and wipes. With the exception of wipes, these effects can be produced in-camera as well as on an optical printer. Film wipes, however, require an optical printer.

• The exits and entrances implied by these effects are secondary to their function as space-time transition devices. Nor should they be used as substitutes when clean entrances and exits are clearly called for.

CHAPTER 11

BUILDUP

THE XYZ'S OF CONTINUITY

This chapter on *buildup* marks an important milestone along the route of continuity study, and we may well pause for a quick RS of the road we have just traveled.

Thus far we have been proceeding along a pretty clearly marked highway, where deviations from the straight and narrow have been inadvisable. Up to this point we have talked in specific terms about the structure of the sequence, about the mechanics of smoothness, coherence, and camera logic. These have been highly practical, hard-and-fast matters, with pointers and warnings and rulings; they have been the fundamentals, the ABC's of pictorial continuity. Now come the XYZ's.

The road ahead is no longer straight or narrow or inadvisable to stray from. It is wide open—broad as the horizon. It has guides for you, the cameraman, but the real progress will depend on your creative imagination, on your "feel" for motion pictures, on that intuitive extra something that can set your work apart.

We have studied pictorial continuity in terms of achieving smooth, coherent action. Now let us apply it to get good story coverage, to create audience interest, to inject variety and color into the trite and ordinary. Buildup is what does this. It puts the frosting on the movie cake.

We have described buildup by indirection, in terms of similes and metaphors. It cannot be contained in a rigid definition, but it may be broadly defined as *the use of secondary shots or sequences which are subordinate to the main action but round out and enrich a story by giving it meaning, clarity, suspense, and excitement.* Although such shots are but modifiers of the main action, they are truly indispensable to complete coverage.

That's quite a chunk of definition. Let's look at it in pictorial terms—your assignment is to shoot a news documentary of a famous hostess's garden party.

The story breaks down easily into sequences. The first one establishes the hostess and the locale—the back lawn, with its grass, flowers, summer furniture and sun umbrellas. People enter the scene. They are greeted, served refreshments, introduced to others. You shoot special sequences of punch being served, of guests consuming sandwiches, of someone playing a musical instrument, of card games, the awarding of prizes and other events; and, finally, of the party breaking up.

You now have a simple story containing most of the action common to all garden parties. You are going to introduce buildup to round it out, pep it up. You will seek out revealing, colorful details, shoot lots of closeups. These shots can be treated as inserts to be filmed out of sequence when the opportunity offers, and placed in proper continuity during editing.

In your opening sequence you make sure that you get shots which emphasize the gala nature of the event and the fact that is is a bright, sunshiny day. If there are flags or streamers, you take shots of them snapping in the breeze. You shoot the glasses neatly lined up by the punchbowl, the trays of cookies, candies and sandwiches. You get quick shots of the hostess hastily touching up decorations before the guests arrive; and perhaps her young children looking wide-eyed at the lavish preparations.

When the guests arrive, you look for details of dress which command attention. A woman may be wearing a fantastic straw hat featuring a figure of a bird pecking at cherries. You shoot a closeup of this and perhaps precede—or follow—it by another CU of a child's eyes popping at the sight. (This CU is known as a *reaction* shot because it is the direct result of the action of a preceding or following scene. A reaction shot is very good for building up dramatic interest. Having it precede the action which causes it is a simple device for creating suspense.)

Instead of shooting the arrival of each guest, you make a series of buildup inserts of the hostesses's hand (recognizable by its distinctive dress sleeve and ring) shaking several different hands, easily identifiable as male, female, or child. This series of buildup shots suggests a number and variety of guests, saves footage, and gives a new slant to the prosaic, everyday business of shaking hands. When a courtly European gentleman kisses her hand, you frame the hostesses's hand in a close shot; in comes the gentleman's hand to grasp hers, followed by his face as he puts his lips to her fingers.

In the refreshments sequence, you take pains to get full-frame CU's and other shots of the punch being poured; then as a tray is passed and the glasses are removed from it one by one, you follow a particular glass with the camera, show it traveling up to a guest's mouth, being tipped over and emptied, and close with the satisfied expression of the drinker.

As for the musical sequence, a typical buildup would be shots of a player's hands as they thrum the guitar strings or press the keys of an accordion.

For the card parties or games you lay stress via closeups or angles on the tiny scenes or bits of action that give point and punch to the sequence: the winning card hand, a chess piece being moved on the board, the reactions of the players—one nervously puffing a cigarette, another wiping his glasses.

In your departure sequence, you pay attention to a lady carefully pinning her hat into her hair; the courtly gentleman's old-fashioned spats, his shoes, and the tip of his cane moving down the walk; the gate opening and closing as one by one the guests leave; wheels of different cars turning as they move away. Returning to the garden, you get buildup in the litter and disorder that characterize the end of the party: quick shots of the empty chairs, the drained punchbowl, the soiled plates, the dog getting an accumulation of scraps, the servants, and perhaps the children collecting debris, under the supervision of the hostess who is now wearing a house apron that contrasts sharply with her elegant party dress; concluding with shots of the flowers, now dull and indistinct in the fading light, and the streamers whose limpness and quiet suggest that they too are exhausted by the activities of the day.

This description of garden party buildup shots, long as it is, touches only the highlights, the more obvious examples of the buildup material contained in a familiar story. Most of your movies wil be equally familiar ones: activities of family and friends in their homes, in the garden, on the tennis court, on picnics, at the beach.

All such subjects are commonplace, but the cameraman who learns to use buildup artfully can make them stimulating and engrossing. Familiar as they are, they can usually supply enough colorful detail and action to give you buildup material.

The poorest motion-picture story will always be improved by buildup. It is up to the cameraman to cultivate it carefully.

WHEN BUILDUP IS ESSENTIAL

The need for buildup is most acute when shooting a static subject where there is no movement of the main action in or out of the frame, or when shooting a story whose main action has already taken place.

For an example, take that inevitable subject for a home movie—baby's bath. It has surefire visual material, but it is also a relatively static subject.

To keep it lively and varied, you should use a wide variety of buildup angles and cuts: a full-frame CU of the soap as the mother's hand reaches into the frame and picks it up; another full-screen closeup of her hand as it adjusts the water temperature or scrubs baby with a washcloth; baby's feet kicking up a foamy sea in the tub; baby's hands playing with rubber toys; baby's grins and hand-clappings of pleasure.

If you combine this sequence with one on drying and dressing the baby, you reestablish first with an MS showing the transfer of the child from her bath to the top of the bathinette, and then give punch to the action with buildup shots of baby being scrubbed dry, oil being poured and rubbed in, powder being sprinkled, diapering, pinning, and dressing. Attention is focused, by means of CU's and angle shots, on graphic details like the oil, powder, safety pins, along with the smiling reactions of baby and mother.

These brief scenes used here and there in rapid succession will give the simple story a snap and lift that are sure to bring "oh!s" and ah!s" from your audience.

Buildup will do the same sort of job in filling out a story whose main action has already taken place. Suppose you hurry to a neighborhood fire, only to find that the firemen have it under control. Its most spectacular phase is over, but you can still make interesting sequences through the use of buildup.

This you find in shots of the occupants driven into the street clutching a few belongings (a chance for inserts); in details of charred debris from the burning building; in the police holding back the crowds; in ambulance attendants, the faces of the spectators, the activity of welfare organizations like the Salvation Army handing out coffee and doughnuts, the action of the engine pump, in angle shots of firemen on ladders or spraying water, of firemen's hands coupling hose or turning a water hydrant valve, of the hose swelling as water surges through it.

The main action must be caught the moment it takes place, for it is hardly likely, in such a wildly uncontrolled subject as a fire, to repeat itself. But there is much more flexibility in the matter of buildup shots; there are usually several opportunities to take the same buildup scene, and action is often controlled. And remember, no single one of your buildup shots is—unlike the main action—really indispensable. If you miss a good buildup scene and can't get another crack at it later on, you can usually find a different one just as interesting.

No camera subject, however seemingly poor, dull, or lifeless, is completely devoid of buildup material. It can be found even in an empty room. Returning to an earlier example, before Mr. Producer enters his office, the camera can take the empty room and tell a full story about him by searching out the objects and knick-knacks on his desk alone.

In any scene, patience and an inquiring eye are bound to turn up promising shots. The important thing is to be on the lookout for them. They are what give originality to your picture and stamp it with *your* individuality as a cameraman.

BUILD UP ACTION SEQUENCES TOO!

We have said a good deal about building up ordinary static—even dull subjects. Do not infer from this that lively subjects do not need buildup.

In the normal run of a cameraman's luck, you are bound to run across subjects crammed with buildup material, running over with action, colorful detail, human interest. Yet even with rich subjects, the tendency is to err far more often in the direction of too little buildup than too much.

Even if you are lucky enough to catch that four-alarm fire just as the first wisps of smoke come drifting out of the building you should not concentrate exclusively on the spectacular scenes of the fire at its height, with flames and smoke everywhere and firemen rescuing trapped occupants in breathtaking style. These are wonderful shots, of course, undeniably the high points of your picture, but in concentrating wholly on them you are likely to ignore those less breathtaking buildup shots—the belongings of the inhabitants, firemen handling the hose, the faces of spectators.

These spectacular shots are peak shots of the action, all right, but they are peak shots *by virtue of contrast* with the less spectacular buildup ones, and you will be sadly disappointed with audience reaction if you show it only the former without the latter.

Your audience will gasp, no doubt, but it will also feel a definite letdown. People don't live with their emotions perpetually keyed to the high pitch your exciting shots demand. Your audience has to be aroused, informed, led up to a climax of feeling to match the climax of interest provided by your spectacular shots.

Avoid jumping straight into the heart of a movie story; develop interest and comprehension; let your audience warm up first by seeing buildup shots.

CUT-INS AND CUT-AWAYS IN FULL GLORY

The heart of buildup, the main sources of those incidental shots which are "subordinate to the main action but round out a story," are cut-ins and cut-aways.

We have defined and described them; we have seen them applied in directional continuity to mask direction changes: but it is now, in their buildup role, that cut-ins and cut-aways come into their real glory, and their endless varied uses are fully exploited.

A simple example shows how they contribute to buildup. Look at your own back yard, where Johnny is mowing the lawn and his pal Freddy is raking the grass and carrying it away.

You shoot a regular sequence to depict the main action, then shoot inserts of the lawnmower in operation, filling your frame with the moving wheels, the blades, the cut grass as it comes spurting from the machine. These inserts are the buildup, explaining the nature of the action more fully, invigorating it with intimate, graphic details. There is Johnny himself. There are opportunities for

BUILDUP
By Using Cut-ins and Cut-aways

Establishing Shot
Medium Shot
Cut-in
Cut-in

Closeup
Reestablishing Shot
Cut-in
Cut-away

cut-ins of his hands guiding the mower, of his mocassin-shod feet as they follow the machine, of his cheerful expression as he pauses a moment from work.

And take a look at Freddy. Both he, as a live actor, and the inanimate tools of his work—the rake and basket—offer excellent possibilities for buildup cut-ins. Get full-frame closeups of Freddy as he bends to his task, or make a shot of his shirt bunching around his waist. Shoot another sequence on Johnny as he begins to tire, with CU's of his dragging feet and weary expression; then return to Freddy for a sequence on the new action of filling the basket, giving it color with inserts of the rake in action collecting a mound of grass, his hands dumping the grass into the basket, and the filled basket itself.

All these are buildup shots, lending color, humor, interesting detail to the bare bones of the main action.

Head-on and tail-away shots can add a sparkling note to buildup. They would be interesting novelty shots in the Johnny-Freddy sequence, *whether or not* they were used to mask changes in screen direction.

Cut-ins and cut-aways, head-ons and tail-aways, are a blessing to the TV news editor. Through them he can build even the briefest sequence into an acceptable picture story. You have undoubtedly seen numerous parades or dedication ceremonies in the newsreels, where stereotyped action was enlivened by cut-ins of the participants and cut-aways of the spectators.

In these pages, we have fitted cut-ins and cut-aways into their proper place in the subject of buildup. We will return soon and repeatedly to them, for without them buildup is impossible.

ANGLES IN BUILDUP

Angles have been recommended for their value in avoiding the continuity fault of jumpy action between shots as well as for the variety they bring to pictures. We now pay tribute to their services in buildup.

Shoot Johnny from a high angle looking down on him: his squat, foreshortened figure seems sunk into the ground, performing a piddling, dull, undramatic job. Or shoot him approaching from a distant at a flat, head-on angle; his progress seems slow, leisurely.

But shoot Johnny from a low angle which frames him against the sky. Then he'll appear to be performing an exciting, herculean task. Or take a close shot from a right angle—he'll seem to zip through his job.

There is nothing quite like a change of angle in motion pictures to stimulate and sustain interest, to make something "new" out of a well-known, familiar subject—whether it is his father watching a football game on TV, mother vacuuming the rug, or Johnny picking out a tune on his guitar.

In pictorial continuity there can be too much of a good thing. The human eye tires very easily of sameness. A change of angle gives it the stimulus it must repeatedly get to maintain attention.

This need is most compelling in a short series of cut-ins or cut-aways of the same action: They pall if seen more than once or twice from the same angle. If your first cut-in of Johnny's lawnmower throwing out grass is taken from the side, next try a tail-away rear view from the ground level, or shoot from above the mower looking down and back as the grass blades zip from the revolving shears.

These different angles, by constantly presenting new aspects of the same subject, keep building it up to ever higher levels of audience enjoyment.

Cut-ins, cut-aways, and angles: these are the guides to buildup.

Nothing more dramatically illustrates the buildup power of these shots than a series of brief, pictorially unrelated insert scenes cut together to form a so-called *montage*—or series of montages. The shots in a montage do not have pictorial continuity, but they have story or idea continuity. They relate to the same theme or make the same point.

Suppose you shoot a story of a family weekend excursion; let's say a camping trip. You establish the theme with a sequence on father, mother and son examining pictures of various camp sites in a travel brochure and making their selection.

Next, you want to convey the hustle and bustle of preparations for the trip. Here's where a montage can be used to advantage. You shoot brief close shots or CUs of the father's hands testing the reel of his fishing rod, the mother's hand preparing sandwiches and the boy's hands loading his camera. Then, more close shots of a food hamper as a thermos bottle is placed in it, sleeping bags being dumped on the floor of the camper, the cap on the car's gas tank being removed and a fuel hose nozzle inserted.

These shots are extremely short, so short that sometimes the action is not even completed—mother's hand is cut in mid-stroke as it butters a slice of bread or the fueling shot is cut before the nozzle is fully inserted in the gas tank.

Or the departure can be visualized through close pan shots of moving feet: dad's wading boots approaching the car's front door which opens to his offscreen hand and the boots start to get in; then panning to the rear door, already open, as mother's field oxfords enter the car, followed by Junior's sneakers. The camera holds its position as the door is closed, the car starts, the rear wheel rolls in and out of the scene in a close shot, then the lower part of the camper. As this vehicle moves out of the scene, the camera pans with it and holds in a tail-away shot.

Buildup through montage sequences contributes to a visual story in various ways: the succession of crisp images imparts drama to even minor story details; the close shots or CUs give them added vividness; their brevity—even to the point of cutting into action—creates an exciting tempo.

And despite the lack of normal pictorial continuity, the audience is never lost or confused; it knows what those visually unrelated shots are all about as long as they are tied together in advance by a sequence that establishes the theme, as the travel brochure sequence does for the camping trip.

A montage is a visual spectacular. It should be used sparingly lest it palls on an audience as any visual excess will do. We respectfully suggest you go back to the first chapter, which spells out the dangers of excessive use of closeups.

CURBING UNCONTROLLED ACTION

When you're shooting uncontrolled or unpredictable action, you can save the situation with cut-ins and cut-aways.

Suppose you want to shoot baby toddling across the living room to where mother is waiting with open arms. You know that the child's attempts at walking are full of hesitations and distractions. You can save yourself a lot of footage if, after shooting the child beginning its walk, you make full frame cut-ins of its moving feet, plus cut-aways of mother's face and her arms outstretched to baby; then stop shooting and wait until the child is within arm's length of mother before starting the camera again for a full shot of the action.

Caution: When using buildup shots of this type like the closeups of baby's moving feet, watch your screen direction! Make sure it is the same as the screen direction in the establishing shot.

SUSPENSE AND EXCITEMENT

Buildup can do remarkable things to audience emotions. One of its most valued abilities is to create curiosity, suspense, and excitement, to send a tingle up the spine, to cause the audience to watch the screen in fascination and wonder anxiously what will follow.

Contrasting screen direction is one way of building an atmosphere of anticipation or tension. So are other forms of cross-cutting, especially in chase sequences. However, you don't need strong action or movement to build up suspense by cross-cutting. It can be used to create suspense by tying together relatively static actions. Suppose you began the Trudy-Dean sequence with both at home preparing for the tennis blind date. If you cut back and forth between Trudy putting on her makeup and Dean brushing his hair, trimming his moustache, etc., you'll instill their mood of anticipation in the audience.

Still another approach to buildup is this: Any action not immediately explained to the audience will create suspense. Your audience will not mind—it will enjoy its puzzlement—if you keep the question mark element interesting and explain it eventually in a satisfying manner.

Introducing a subject or part of a subject in a big closeup will always create suspense. (When using a CU deliberately for this purpose, let the scene run longer than usual—don't make a quick cut of it.) With this in mind, let us try reshooting that simple sequence of Mr. Producer.

Instead of having an LS first, you shoot a big, frame-filling CU of his hands engaged in writing, or perhaps of his eyes staring into or beyond the camera. (Staring into the camera, even in a big, dominating closeup, is all right as long as the eyes do not betray *awareness of the camera*. In other words, the subject should "look right through it.") Your audience, seeing those tremendous CU's of hands or eyes would immediately ask: Whose are they? Just what are the eyes looking at? What are the hands writing?

In the LS and MS scenes that follow you provide the explanation. As your camera pulls back in order to show the relationship of those eyes or hands to the general scene, the audience sees that Mr. Producer is reading a letter or writing a check.

Now the familiar routine of LS, MS, and CU is completely mixed up. But that order of shots has never been termed unchangeable. It *is* the best method of telling a simple story clearly. But when you want to introduce suspense and excitement, it is perfectly allowable to juggle the order around.

Only don't sell suspense cheaply! In the case of Mr. Producer, it's something of a letdown to find that those big, staring eyes in your closeup have been looking at nothing more exciting than a form letter. Suppose you follow that CU with an MS of him at his desk, still staring beyond the camera. If you take a reverse-angle LS that reveals a man standing in the doorway and holding, not a script, but a gun pointed at Mr. Producer, you have justifiably varied routine to create suspense.

Suspense can also be produced by the extreme opposite of violent action, by a scene without any action at all. Open your picture with a sleeping figure; you immediately create curiosity about who the person is, plus where he is, and why he or she is there. Put a troubled or joyous expression on that sleeping person's face, and audience suspense soars as it looks forward to learning the reason for the expression.

You can have suspense without any actor in the scene at all. Open up with Mr. Producer's office before anyone walks in; your audience looks forward to seeing what manner of person will enter. Move in on some specific object in that empty room, such as a pile of scripts or a telegram on his desk. Audience suspense grows sharp in anticipation of the drama that will unfold when the objects are explained.

Suspense does not need the extreme of high drama to justify it. It is also well employed for humorous effect. Suppose you opened the lawn-mowing sequence with a cut-in of a pair of feet. They move slowly, wearily. They suggest the extreme exhaustion of a man who has been on his feet traveling for many hours and many miles—a hiker or a woodsman, perhaps a refugee or a criminal. Then you pull back the camera to an LS and those tired feet are disclosed as belonging to Johnny pushing the lawnmower. You've got a sure-fire laugh.

Obviously, when you're building up suspense by camera movement, a continuous moving shot like a dolly-in—or a zoom-in—may be more effective than a succession of shots. Since the shot is continuous, audience attention remains uninterrupted.

Suppose, in your MS, Mr. Producer picked up that now notorious gun and pointed it at you. To keep the audience eye fixed on the lethal object and deliberately not give it a chance to relax, you dolly or zoom in instead of cutting to a CU, until the weapon fills the entire screen.

Conversely, a dolly- or zoom-back can do an equally effective job in keeping your audience in the grip of suspense. Open your sequence with a CU or an ECU of the screen-filling gun pointed right at the audience. Then move back to reveal it is Mr. Producer who holds the gun; continue to move back and we see that the object of his wrath is a saleman who just can't take "no" for an answer.

Trucking shots to follow action often create memorable visual excitement. They are virtually bread-and-butter shots in police stories, war films or westerns when the attack or the chase is on.

Try an example back home—a bicycle race between Junior and his friend. A close follow shot of Junior as he pedals for dear life will delight you and your audience with the feeling of suspense it creates.

CONTRAST

Contrast—for drama or comedy—is heightened by those versatile cut-ins and cut-aways. Consider this example: You're planning to shoot a story from your car of your son jogging in his first running shoes. You can add a lot of buildup appeal with an introductory sequence at home. It opens with his putting on one of the running shoes, goes to a closeup of the shoes; then dissolves to a montage of CUs of earlier footwear. There are the baby booties his mother insisted on keeping, his first little-boy laced shoes and—as he continued to grow—progressively larger-sized sneakers, loafers, hiking boots, dress shoes, etc. Dissolve back to his putting on the other running shoe, a closeup as he ties the laces, then neatly match cut to your outdoor story of the running shoes pounding the road, etc.

That immediately suggests an opposite kind of contrast sequence. You want to show the delicacy, the tiny size of your little girl. So you give the camera to mother and have her shoot you taking daughter for a walk. She will, of course, take closeups of daughter's little fingers clasped in your brawny fist and, of course, her diminutive shoes trying to keep pace with your size 11 brogans.

Contrast buildup comes in all sizes and shapes. How about adding a touch of humor to the lawnmower sequence? Cross-cut a cut-in of the mower shearing the grass with a closeup of your razor as you draw it through the lather on your face, and so on.

Contrast material is present in nearly every subject or action, a powerful challenge to the imaginative powers of the cameraman. It is a most rewarding challenge, though, not only for the personal satisfaction which effective use of contrast will give, but also for the pleasure it will bring an audience.

A movie audience is acutely susceptible to the power of suggestion. Contrast has a great deal of that power.

Don't be discouraged when you gamble on an effect of contrast that doesn't quite come off. That will happen occasionally; it's part of the price you must pay to gain experience. You'll learn by observing audience reaction. Once you have learned not to overreach, and your contrast does come off successfully, the warm response it receives will more than compensate for any previous failures.

LIGHTING IN BUILDUP
AND CONTINUITY

Neither this book on continuity nor this chapter on buildup would be quite complete without a word about lighting.

Lighting has strong dramatic value. Even such simple shifts in light source as back-lighting or side-lighting give a more interesting picture than lighting from a flat angle.

The professional cinematographer, skilled in the intricacies of the craft, can maniplate the entire lighting scheme of a scene to express varying emotions that exert a powerful influence on a movie audience. Low-key lighting, with its pronounced contrast in light and shadow, creates a somber, intensely dramatic mood. High-key lighting, with its abundance of illumination, is conducive to a cheerful state of mind.

The non-professional should be extremely cautious about attempting to use lighting for buildup, especially in interior scenes. It is a true art, complicated and subtle, calling for study and experience. But fortunately for the non-professional, too short of time to delve into lighting profundities, most home subjects are of an outdoor nature. Fortunately too, the indoor movie themes are usually cheerful and pleasant, calling merely for adequate illumination to get a good exposure.

The great concern of the non-professional, therefore, should be *continuity of lighting*—making sure that the lighting of related scenes is reasonably consistent.

If you're shooting that little girl indoors under artificial light, make sure that your lighting of the cut-ins is reasonably identical with the lighting for the main shots.

Suppose, in that lawn-mowing epic, you wish to make a complete sequence of Freddy carrying a basket filled with cut grass over to a large disposal can and dumping it. If the sun is dodging in and out of clouds, wait to make your different shots in the sequence for those moments when the sun's brightness is about the same.

Be particularly careful, when your story supposedly covers a long period of time, that the lighting jibes with the facts. If you're making a comic movie of Johnny painting the doghouse and want to emphasize his extremely slow progress by frequent inserts of a wristwatch to show the lapse of many hours, don't let lighting betray you! The sun is always moving, and s sharp-eyed spectator in your audience would get mighty suspicious if he didn't see the shadow cast by the doghouse in a different place with each return to the main action. (One could get around the problem, of course, by shooting this particular story on a dull day when no shadows at all are cast.)

The question of the movement of the sun brings us to another important aspect of lighting continuity: consistency of the main source of light.

You are shooting Johnny as he lies on the lawn, relaxing from his arduous painting labors. Side light is striking his face so that your LS and MS in this sequence show half his face in shadow. You move in for a CU from the same angle. This shot should show the same distribution of light and shadow. Don't have him turn between shots to get the light fully on both sides of his face unless you show the action. Unless your movie audience sees him make the move, the lighting inconsistency will be obvious. If you think the CU shows his face too dark on one side, go back and reshoot your MS with his face more fully illuminated, either by having him shift his position or by using a reflector.

Of course, when Johnny has resumed his work and is moving around once more, he will constantly keep shifting his position in regard to the light source; his *movement* will account for variations in the play of light on his person.

The temptation to overlook consistency of light source is especially strong when shooting indoors with photofloods, where the cameraman has complete control of his light sources and can shift them at will. You are shooting a sequence of mother rocking baby to sleep in her cradle. The main source of light is a photoflood placed to favor baby, with the result that mother's face is partly in shadow during the LS and MS. Don't—if you take a big CU of mother—shift your light so that her face is fully illumined unless the MS shows her moving into a more favorable position.

Consistency of the lighting source, in sum, calls for careful attention to the logical requirements of your story.

Another element to consider in the matter of lighting continuity is that of consistency of light *quality*.

If you're shooting under artificial light, over which you have complete control, there should be no problem. It's a different story when you're shooting outdoors, especially in the case of color film. The quality of light varies according to the time of day because the color temperature of light changes. Early morning light is reddish, late afternoon light even more so.

This variability of light quality can be compensated for by the use of corrective filters; also color negative can be corrected in the lab during printing. Of course you won't bother with color correction if you *want* to show that a particular scene is being enacted in the early morning or late afternoon. Then you'll encourage those reddish hues.

Another problem arises when an outdoor sequence which may run only a few minutes onscreen, is actually shot over a matter of days. Obviously light quality should be uniform throughout the sequence. But one day may be bright and sunny, producing sharply defined shadows and high image contrast; while the next day may be overcast, with diffused shadows and much lower contrast! Drastic variations like these make it impossible to match the light quality of scenes shot on different days.

If you're shooting a home movie, waiting for a day when light quality matches an earlier day is a nuisance. If you're shooting a feature movie, the delay means much more; it means a jump in production costs. In either case there's not much you can do except beseech the weatherman to be kind.

A basic caution when shooting outdoors is to avoid pointing a video camera at the sun accidentally. This can damage the tube or sensor. Keep the lens cap on between shots![44]

THE ULTIMATE COMPLIMENT

The ultimate compliment to be paid buildup is the fact that it gives the camera one of its rare opportunities to triumph over the human eye.

Buildup develops, controls, and speeds up interest in what the audience eye sees in a way that the human eye in real life simply cannot do as efficiently.

The eye in real life easily gets bored. It will look with interest at what it sees for the first time, but will soon wander off in search of something else when the object of its attention turns dull and repetitious. The human eye is constantly engaged—outside the theatre—in the task of *selecting* what is interesting from the many commonplace scenes it encounters every moment of the day.

Had your audience seen Johnny and Freddy at work in real life, it would have watched with interest those actions which were novel and seen for the first time: the mower in motion, the cut grass raked together. But the moment those actions were repeated more than once or twice—as they must be—its eye would instinctively wander off in search of something new to look at.

Shrewdly built-up continuity spares the audience this monotony of excessive repetition and avoids the real-life strain of searching for "something different" to see.

It does so by pre-selecting footage that is consistently new and interesting, by concentrating attention through vivid full-frame cut-ins and cut-aways on the important phases of an action, and, with a change of angle, by creating a fresh point of view and stimulating interest anew.

Here we see the trimph of illusion. Surely real life is never as consistently absorbing and free of ennui as motion-picture buildup can make it!

SUMMARY

Buildup "makes" a picture by injecting variety and color into the trite and ordinary.

• Buildup is the use of secondary shots or sequences which are subordinate to the main action but which round out a story by giving it meaning, clarity, suspense, and excitement.

• The need for buildup is most acute when shooting a static subject where there is no movement in or out of the frame; or when shooting a story whose main action has already taken place.

• Action sequences, as well as static or dull subjects, should be built up. The full effect of exciting shots is lost unless audience anticipation is led up to them by means of buildup.

• Cut-ins and cut-aways are the core of buildup. They are its most important, most flexible, richest source of material.

• Angles play an important part in buildup shots.

• Buildup shots are also useful in curbing uncontrolled action.

• Buildup shots can convey an idea very dramatically in the form of a *montage*—a series of brief close shots that do not have pictorial continuity but convey the same idea.

• Contrast is an important buildup element for comedy or drama.

• Proper lighting can make a major contribution to buildup but it must be handled with genuine expertise, especially in the case of interior lighting.

• Make sure there is continuity of lighting in related scenes; and, consistency of *light quality* as well.

CHAPTER 12

TRANSITIONS IN TIME AND SPACE

JUGGLING TIME AND SPACE

One of the magical powers of a motion picture is its ability to juggle time and space—to be both time machine and magic carpet for an audience. This power of illusion rests on skillful transitions to cover jumps in time and space. Cut-ins and cut-aways are invaluable to this end. They can span any amount of time or distance smoothly and convincingly, swiftly or slowly, as the film maker desires.

How often have you seen cut-aways of falling calendar leaves or successive shots of the same clock to indicate the rapid passage of time? or a clock used to make the passage of five minutes seem like hours, by means of repeated cut-aways to the minute hand as it slowly crawls from point to point? Hundreds of thousands of miles are bridged by successive shots of an automobile odometer, by cut-ins of car wheels spinning rapidly, by passing from a shot of snowy mountains to a scene of a sun-kissed beach!

Let's analyze this magical power to condense time and space, using the lawn-mowing sequence as an example. Suppose you want a "before and after" version of the lawn. Your opening shot shows it overgrown with grass; your closing shot pictures it neatly clipped.

A lot of lawn-mowing lies between those two shots—quite a bit of time and space has been covered. You haven't enough footage to shoot all that grass-cutting, and what's more important, the action would eventually get repetitious and boring no matter what means you employed to distract the audience.

The solution lies in cut-ins of Johnny mowing and cut-aways of Freddy raking. You simply take these cuts and judiciously spread them among your shots of the main action, which consist of regular LS's and MS's of the boys busy at work. Then the whole cutting and raking operation, which actually takes an hour to perform, can be condensed to a minute and your audience will have the impression of watching a full, complete lawn-mowing job. Cut-ins and cut-aways will have concealed the time lapses.

JUGGLING TIME AND SPACE

Reestablishing Shot
Cut-in
Closeup
Reestablishing Shot

Cut-in
Closeup
Reestablishing Shot
Cut-away

The psychological secret that explains the audience's acceptance of this quick passage of time is the same continuity truism that an audience rarely thinks back beyond the scene prior to the one at which it is looking. Cut-ins and cut-aways provide interesting distraction from the main action. When you *do* return to the main action, your audience readily accepts the idea that a good many things have happened, that considerable time has passed and considerable ground has been covered in the interval.

If your opening shots showing Johnny starting the mowing are followed by full-frame cut-ins of his moving feet, each taken from a different angle, even though these scenes are short and few in number, the audience will accept a succeeding long or medium shot which shows Johnny far away from his starting point and with a great deal of the lawn already trimmed. Likewise with Freddy, once you've established him putting the cut grass in a basket, you can return to it a few shots later for a closeup showing it half-filled; then return again after a brief interval for another CU showing the basket heaped full. In real time, this process would take quite a while; in screen time, it is just a matter of seconds.[45]

In both instances, the passage of time and space has been convincingly *implied.* By using cut-ins and cut-aways of this nature throughout the sequence, you carry your audience unjarred over big jumps in time and space up to the final scene, which shows the lawn completely cut and raked, and the boys walking off with their tools.

Cut-aways are even more effective than cut-ins for putting over such an illusion. The reason is that they depict a subject completely separate physically from the main action. Audience distraction, consequently, is more complete. The perfect cut-aways for the lawn-mowing story would be shots of Johnny's mother smiling at the two landscape artists; also a shot of the dog frisking about.

The illusion is always greater if you use several short shots of a subject taken from different angles instead of just a single shot. For instance, if you first showed a medium shot of the mother knitting or reading; then a closer angle as she looks up and smiles approvingly at the boys offscreen. Every time you change to a different shot—no matter how brief—you introduce a new idea into the mind of your audience.

PICTORIAL TRANSITIONS FROM PLACE TO PLACE

The lawn-mowing sequence illustrates how time and space can be condensed in one particular location or place. Suppose, however, you want to add a sequence showing the boys enjoying themselves at an ice cream parlor; in other words, a jump in space from one place to another some distance away. The right cut-in or cut-away can provide a pictorial transition shot—or shots—to bridge the gap convincingly and with eye appeal.

Here's one way of doing it: you end the lawn-mowing sequence by show-ing Johnny's mother handing over the ice cream money and the boys leaving on their bikes. For a transition shot, shoot a cut-in of a revolving bike wheel and you have an easy, swift and strongly pictorial transition between the two sequences. When suitable to the story, pictorial transitions should be action shots rather than static ones.

But we can also have an effective space-time transition without the use of a connecting shot such as the bicycle wheel. Go back to mother giving Johnny the ice cream money. Make the last shot in the sequence a CU of Johnny's outstretched hand as mother's hand enters the frame to drop a dollar into Johnny's palm, then withdraws out of frame. We follow this shot with another closeup of Johnny's hand—with the money in it—but this time the other hand that enters the scene—a distinctively different, masculine one—takes the dollar. The next scene, an MS, shows the boys to be in the ice cream parlor and the strange hand taking the money is that of the soda clerk![46]

This, too, is a strong action transition, even though it doesn't have the movement of the turning wheels. And take note that it was done through the use of cut-in shots.

This kind of pictorial transition is known as *matching action,* but do not confuse it with the matching action used in overlap to avoid jump cuts!

(Matching action between two transition shots calls for two similar-appear-ing actions by two different subjects, both shot from the *same angle*; overlap involves *two different angles* of the same action performed by the same sub-ject. Take another look at the opening pages of Chapter 4).[47]

It might be said that the hands transition is more dramatic from a story viewpoint while the revolving bike wheel is pictorially more exciting. And because the hands transition involves matching action, it has tighter pictorial continuity.

That's not to say that either transition is better or preferable. The choice is up to the moviemaker, based on what effect he's trying to accomplish through his images onscreen. The point is there are different ways of getting an effec-tive pictorial transition as long as the moviemaker exercises his motion picture imagination. As we've said before, pictorial continuity is highly flexible; methods for achieving it are many and varied.[48]

TIME-SPACE TRANSITIONS
BY MECHANICAL EFFECTS

Transitions in space and time can be made on film by the fade-out, fade-in, the dissolve, the blur pan, blur focus shot and the wipe. These effects were discussed earlier in relation to clean exits and entrances, but their primary and most important use is to make space-time transitions between scenes and sequences.

A fade-out closes or locks up a scene with unarguable finality; a fade-in ushers in a brand new beginning. A considerable span of space and time can be covered between the two shots without disturbing the audience in the least, as long as there is a logical connection between them.

An example would be to fade out on the lawn-mowing story with a shot of Johnny's mother giving him and Freddy some spending money for their labors, then fade in to show the boys enjoying themselves in an ice cream parlor. Not only would the audience accept this swift passage of time and space, it would find the transition from hard work to complete relaxation an amusing contrast.

The same psychology applies to the dissolve. It could be used very nicely to bridge the shots between the final lawn scene and the ice cream parlor. A dissolve is especially effective when used to show different time readings. Dissolving from closeup to closeup of the mother's wristwatch during the lawn-mowing sequence would suggest the passage of considerable time.[49]

What a mechanical transition does is to give the audience a very brief—almost subliminal—signal that the film story is making a jump in time and/or space. Recognizing the signal, the audience accepts the jump without feeling there has been a gap in continuity.

The blur pan, blur focus and wipe operate the same way. These mechanical effects can also be used for the time/space transition of the boys from the lawn-mowing sequence to the ice cream parlor.

But be warned: Use mechanical transition effects sparingly. They are, after all, artificial devices and you don't want to clutter up your film with them. It's poor workmanship, like pounding too many nails into a cabinet you're building or using unnecessary stitches in a garment you're sewing. And *don't* try to use mechanical transitions to take the curse off faulty continuity or uninteresting action. You'll never deceive an audience that way.

When you feel a mechanical transition is in order, be judicious in the kind you choose. A blur pan might be fine to connect two fast-moving sequences in an action story; it would be visual "overkill" to show a woman cutting some flowers in her garden then blur panning to inside her living room where she is seen placing the flowers in a vase. Or a flashy wipe might mar the mood of a romantic love story; on the other hand, it might enhance the film if the love story was being told as a comedy of laughable incidents and absurd misunderstandings.

Do these choices seem like an embarrassment of riches? Perhaps you're just starting out as a movie maker and you honestly feel your visual sense is not sufficiently developed to make the right choice. In that case, here's a simple rule of thumb to take you off the hook of decision making: Use the simplest kind of mechanical transition you feel comfortable with. You can't go wrong if you use the simplest of them all—the dissolve.

An even better rule of thumb is to use a pictorial transition whenever possible. It is visually more appealing, more natural and less likely to call attention to itself than a mechanical transition. And it can be a real stimulus to the moviemaker's creativity.

THE STRAIGHT CUT

Most moviemakers today do not use any visual transitional devices at all, either pictorial or mechanical. They prefer a *straight cut* between sequences. For example, they would cut directly from the scene of Johnny and Freddy receiving ice cream money to a scene of the two boys in the ice cream parlor, eating away with gusto.

Advocates of the straight cut say that it makes for a "cleaner," "tighter" and more "natural" transition; that both a pictorial or mechanical transition are unnecessary because the theme and logical development of a film story will carry the audience smoothly from one sequence to another without the use of an "artificial" or "contrived" connecting device; and, last but far from least, that straight cuts speed up tempo.[50]

To debate the merits of the straight cut against those of the pictorial or mechanical transition is fruitless, especially when the debate is carried out in "all or nothing," sweeping generalizations. There are too many instances where the choice can be made on strictly subjective grounds, a matter of the individual moviemaker's taste and "feel" for the medium. "One man's meat, etc. . . ."[51]

A straight cut should be considered as another option in making time/space transitions. However, a straight cut requires special attention to the needs of pictorial continuity. If you haven't prepared the audience for an abrupt change in time or place; if it is needlessly disturbing to the eye; or if it confuses the viewer—even momentarily—as to what is happening, then the straight cut will stand out like a sore thumb, just like a jump cut between shots within a sequence. You will have lost the visual coherence that pictorial continuity is all about; and when you lose that, you start to lose your audience.[52]

WHICH KIND OF TRANSITION?

Now you have a variety of ways of making time/space transitions between sequences. Which one to choose? Obviously the one that provides the smoothest, most "seamless" pictorial continuity. How do you determine whether that is a straight cut, a pictorial transition, or mechanical transition? There is no fixed order or preference, no infallible clues as to which kind of transition to use. You must look for the answer in the visual context of your scenes.

Sometimes the answer is easy. Suppose you're shooting a safety movie in which two drivers are demonstrating the right and wrong way to drive a car; or a documentary or fictional episode in which an ambulance is trying to rush a rare type of blood plasma through heavy traffic while at a hospital a critically ill patient is waiting for the plasma to keep him alive. In both stories you use direct cuts to cross-cut between actions, since it is the most effective transition for creating sharp contrast or maintaining dramatic tension.

There are occasions when a mechanical transition clearly recommends itself as best. This is especially true of an action which is static, repetitious or tedious, but necessary to the story. For example, take a meal sequence in a movie about a typical child's day. The child is lively and attractive in everything it does except at mealtime when it is an irritatingly slow eater. You want to show this to your audience without boring it or slowing down the film tempo too much. So you start shooting the eating sequence and as soon as the child's dawdling is established (including some buildup shots of his exasperated mother), a simple dissolve will provide a smooth transition to a shot of the child brushing its teeth before running out to play.

On the other hand, a nature story filmed in a botanical gardens, or out in the fields or woods with lots of plants and flowers, calls very naturally for pictorial transitions.

But obvious choices are not all that common. Then the moviemaker must put his editorial judgment and creative visual sense to work. That's part of the challenge—and the fun—of moviemaking. And don't get caught in an agony of indecision about which kind of transition to use. If you're honestly in doubt, you're always safe with a pictorial transition. Only don't be afraid to make mistakes in this or any other aspect of pictorial continuity; learn from them. No one is born with instant expertise.[53]

THE SHOCK CUT

Brace yourself. A short while ago we cautioned you that a straight cut should not be needlessly disturbing to the eye. Now we're going to say there are times when it is used deliberately to create an abrupt, jarring visual transition, for the sake of the story. It is then generally described as a *shock cut,* since it is intended to surprise, startle or even frighten the audience.

Suppose you're watching a Florida vacation movie shot by your aforementioned neighbor Mr. Montgomery, who is a very knowledgeable cameraman. His opening sequence features Mrs. Montgomery who is happily packing a suitcase. The very next shot—a straight cut—is a tight closeup of an alligator's wide-open jaws. The audience, including you, couldn't help being shocked by the abrupt transition from pleasureable anticipation to deadly menace. You would not only fear for Mrs. Montgomery, you would actually share her terror if the next shot showed her on a Florida shore with the 'gator moving toward her.

The shock cut can be used in other ways to catch an audience by surprise. Suppose after the closeup of those deadly jaws, Mr. Montgomery pulled back his camera or zoomed back—to show his wife watching the alligator in perfect safety from behind the bars of a protective fence. The audience would sigh in relief or laugh for being so neatly deceived.

So, you see, a straight cut can hit you in the eye, so to speak, without disrupting pictorial continuity; it can play a key role in the visual coherence of the sequences that tell your story.

The shock cut can be used within a sequence as well as a transitional device. To illustrate, let's run back the film or tape to Mrs. Montgomery packing. She finishes and we see her pleased expression in a CU. The next shot is a closeup of a man's grizzled face staring intently. Back to Mrs. M. to show that she is startled, even apprehensive—and so are we. We again see the man, but in a medium shot. He is putting on the taxi driver's cap he had in his hand. We realize—with her—that he is a harmless cabbie hired for the drive to the airport.

Warning: Shock cuts lose impact rapidly when used to excess.

SUMMARY

The juggling of time and space is one of the most powerful illusions a motion picture can create. Cut-ins and cut-aways are invaluable in providing transition shots to cover jumps in time and space.

• Pictorial transitions between sequences involving a jump in space from one place to another some distance away can be done by using a cut-in or cut-away as a connecting shot. Pictorial transitions should use action shots rather than static ones, when suitable to the story.

• Pictorial transitions can also be made by matching action. This should not be confused with overlap.

• Time/space transitions can also be made through the use of mechanical effects such as the fade-out, fade-in, dissolve, blur pan, blur focus shot and the wipe. Mechanical transitions should be used sparingly and carefully.

• Many moviemakers do not use pictorial or mechanical transitions, but prefer a straight cut between sequences. A straight cut should not disrupt pictorial continuity.

• A shock cut is used deliberately to create an abrupt, jarring visual transition in order to surprise, startle, or frighten an audience.

• Shock cuts lose impact when used to excess.

CHAPTER 13

STORY AND EDITING

EDITORIAL JUDGMENT

It is not the province of this book to analyze scenario writing. We are studying pictorial continuity: those rules of structure, logic, and form which work to make a coherent motion picture story regardless of the type of plot, much as certain rules of building construction are applied regardless of whether the building is a cottage or a skyscraper.

But just as rules of building construction do control the flow and movement of people within a structure, so does pictorial continuity have a powerful effect on the development of any plot.

This held true even in the simple sequence of Mr. Producer, where the most emphatic, intensifying shot—the CU—was reserved for his face. In other words, there was a rudimentary scenario entitled "Seeing Mr. Producer" which reached its climax with the closeup. Pictorial continuity was thus closely integrated with story continuity.

As a further example of the logic and laws of common sense they both share, neither pictorial nor plot continuity would allow an LS of Mr. Producer to be followed by an MS of a horse race and then a CU of baby eating her cereal.

The above analogies are elementary views of the correlation between pictorial and story continuity. But with that correlation made clear, we can look further into how pictorial continuity, broadening in scope as it progresses, now touches on a subject that strongly affects the shape and quality of a cameraman's work. That subject is his *editorial judgment*—his control over his picture from the viewpoints of form, emphasis, tempo, content, and final touches.

ADVANCE PLANNING

The ideal motion picture would be subject to the absolute control of the moviemaker blessed with a complete shooting script that he could follow without the slightest deviation. Well, that's pretty much a fantasy wish. Furthermore, many cameramen don't want to be bothered with an elaborately detailed scenario. Shooting a picture—especially for the non-professional—is often a spontaneous act, done on impulse, done to seize an unusual, quickly passing opportunity. It would defeat the purpose and even sour his pleasure to be burdened with a minutely figured plan of action.

So when we recommend some sort of advance planning, we keep the needs of the quick-working type of cameraman in mind. He needn't have a detailed scenario, highly desirable though that might be. He can shoot very effectively without any script at all—"off the cuff" as movie slang puts it—as long as he does "*some mental picture planning in advance.*

What does this mean? Simply that the cameraman before he brings the camera viewfinder up to his eye, makes a mental list of those shots he needs to have his picture coherent and complete; fits in his long, medium, closeup, and reestablishing shots, cut-ins, and the rest according to the importance or dramatic interest of the action; and keeps this mental list fresh in his mind at least two or three shots ahead of the one he is actually taking. Examples follow.

"Boathouse . . .

Assume that a cameraman is going to shoot a story about a city family and the coming of spring. They will celebrate the event by taking a boat ride on the local lake. The cameraman's thoughts might go something like this:

"I think I'll stop on the way to the boathouse at that hill that looks down on the lake and take a location shot from there.

"Then I'll take my regular establishing shot down by the lake from the side of the boathouse, showing part of the building, people lined up to hire boats moored to the dock, and people out on the lake.

"Now I'll get into the meat of my sequence by moving up for a LS of the ticket line with the father—I'll build my story around him—making a clean entrance to join the line. Next, maybe a MS of the cashier selling a ticket to someone, followed by another medium shot of the father waving to his family, and a cut-away of them waving back. Then if I cut back to a MS of the father, I can get away with showing him pretty close to the ticket window. . . .

"Think I'll shoot some more cut-away stuff to get him even closer to the window. I'll take a close shot of him putting up his hand to shade his eyes as he looks in the direction of the lake. Then I'll shoot the lake from his point of view, showing people out on the water. That's good buildup and I'll let the shot run a little long. If it's very colorful I'll zoom in for closer shots of the boaters in canoes and rowboats.

"Time now to get back to the business of buying the ticket. By now the father has moved all the way up to the ticket window. So I'll reestablish with a MS as he steps forward, pulling out his money as he hands it through the window.

"I can get the ticket man into the action with a CU showing him taking the money and stamping the time on a ticker—good idea to get an insert of the stamper doing the job—now I'm all set for an RS as the father picks up the ticket and walks out of the frame to the right in the direction of his family.

"My next shot will be an MS of his wife looking to the left. Her husband enters from screen left; then I'll pan the whole family as they walk off to the boats.

"That's plenty in the way of advance planning before I get there. I can decide on the shots for the next sequence after I finish shooting that one."

Let's assume that the cameraman, by means of that persuasiveness so valuable to a moviemaker, gets the people in the line not to stare at the camera, persuades the ticket man to stamp Junior's ticket over again for an insert cut-in, and in general manages to shoot the sequence pretty much as he had planned it. He does decide to add a few cut-aways of attractive buildup shots he finds in the line—a young sailor and his girl, a kid munching popcorn, a little boy waving a balloon, and as many pretty girls his roving eye—camerawise, that is!—can find.

. . . and Rowboat"

Our cameraman does the same advance picture planning as he prepares to shoot his next sequence which will show the family getting into the rowboat. His mental scenario might call for these shots:

1. LS of mother and Junior approaching rowboat, letting them come cleanly into frame or else dissolving them into head-on shot; then panning them as they come around side of boat and prepare to get in.

2. MS from a different angle as the father gives the mother his hand to help her into the boat.

3. CU of her smiling face.

4. MS to show boat rocking as she steps into it.

5. Another CU of her face as the smile gives way to a gasp of fear.

6. CU of the father laughing at her startled expression.

7. MS cut-away of children reacting.

8. MS to reestablish boat scene as father places his foot on the gunwale of the boat to steady it.

9. CU cut-in of foot.

10. MS from boat (probably a wide-angle shot) as father waves the mother to a seat in the stern.

11. CU of her seating herself and grasping sides of boat.

12. MS from boat to reestablish as the children get into the boat and take seats.

13. MS from dock (a reverse angle) as the father pushes off, seats himself and grasps the oars.

14. MS of father as he begins to row.
15. CU cut-ins of hands working oars.
16. MS of family from father's point of view as mother and children look around.
17. LS of other boats as rowboat moves out into lake.

He continues this advance planning for the sequences that follow, keeping it flexible so that he can change shots, omit or add them—especially cut-aways—to suit the situation when he is actually shooting.

TIPS ON ADVANCE PLANNING

Neither of the example sequences given above need be planned or shot as elaborately as described. Either or both of them could be condensed a great deal, with no loss of continuity, although they would not have quite as much buildup.

Our cameraman might decide that the first sequence being introductory, should move very quickly and therefore will be limited to the essentials of buying a ticket. He confines his picture planning to the following shots: a location shot, an LS of the ticket line as the father joins it, an MS picking him up as he moves to the window and a CU showing him buying the ticket. A reestablishing shot panning him back to his family and remaining focused on the group as they walk down to the boat, would carry the action smoothly into the main boating sequence.

Another important lesson may be drawn from the mental picture planning illustrated by the boating sequences. The lesson is that such planning presupposes, first and foremost, *a clear idea* of what the cameraman is going to shoot, of what his climax will be, and of how he will build up to it.

Naturally this sort of spontaneous scenario planning is much easier with a controlled story in your own living room, or even a semi-controlled story like the boating sequence, than with the wildly uncontrolled story of a raging fire.

But mental picture planning within a sequence is always possible *to some extent,* even when action is wholly uncontrolled. Firemen putting a hose into operation or hurrying up a ladder compose sequences that break down into separate scenes of LSs, MSs, CUs, and ECUs, despite their high speed of action. You can figure in advance on a long shot from across the street as the fire truck rolls up (entering the frame, if possible); then a medium shot as the firemen start to unroll the hose; closeups of the firemen; a reestablishing scene as they drag hose to the water pump; an MS as they start clamping it on; CUs, and ECUs of the hose being tightened.

Similarly, a sequence built around the fire ladder could be tentatively broken down in advance into a long and medium shot of it being raised and placed against the wall; a closeup of the machinery performing the operation and another of the fireman at the controls; an RS of a fireman starting to mount the ladder; a cut-in of his feet as they go up on the rungs; a long shot as he goes into a window.

Obviously, not all of these shots may be possible, especially the close-range, intimate CUs, and ECUs. It must be a carefully obeyed principle with you, as with all responsible cameramen, never to get in the way of people engaged in rescue work at the scene of a disaster. Long lenses, in such instances, can perform the function of close physical approach.

The point to be observed in these examples is that advance planning, no matter how subject to sudden change or cancellation, *can* be done. It is possible for you to *anticipate* scenes *in* uncontrolled action and this anticipation, even if unrealized, can serve as a rough guide in shooting.

The ability to look ahead and anticipate stages of action is a great boon to lightning-quick picture planning, but don't forget that this ability derives from practice and experience.

Just as improvised picture planning is easier when the action is controlled rather than uncontrolled, so it is easier if your movie is simple and brief. Shooting a child eating an ice cream cone is far less complicated than exposing several reels or cassettes on a four-alarm fire. Yet even with the latter, you can correct your mistakes in picture planning by editing afterward.

Here's a final word on advance picture planning. Look at it this way: a housewife finds that shopping for the day is usually more efficient if she plans a list, mental or written, of what she must get at the butcher's, the baker's, the grocer's. Such a list takes only a little while to make up. Advance picture planning need take no more time. The important thing is *to do it.* The habit of it will soon take hold.

Whether you figure out your shots on a mental slate, or scribble a few notes on memo paper, or prefer to work out an elaborate scenario, plan your work in advance as much as possible—before, during, and after shooting.

EDITORIAL JUDGMENT
WHILE SHOOTING

Advance story planning is a vital aspect of editorial judgment. But the planning is still only a means to the shooting. The payoff of your work as a cameraman depends on those powers of camera judgment that put your individual stamp on a picture, that enables you to mark each shot with your own personality.

The answer to this "how," the guides to putting your creative powers to work on a movie, have been suggested in the study of buildup, where concrete details in the form of cut-ins and cut-aways, variety of angles, suspense, contrast, and so on, were called for.

But there are other factors, less exact, more difficult to nail down, calling for a strong exercise of editorial judgment, that play an important point in the quality, the liveliness, the interest of your picture. One of the most elusive and critical of these is tempo.

TEMPO

Tempo, timing, or *pace* are synonymous movie terms that have a rather forbidding sound for the non-professional. The idea of tempo, however, is simple enough. It is the rate of movement, the relative speed or slowness of your motion picture action. The nature of the story is the prime factor in determining tempo. A documentary about an artist putting the finishing touches on a painting has an inherently slower tempo than a sports story about a basketball game. Another factor is the nature of the physical movement. Cars in a drag race move faster than a child pedaling a tricycle.

Tempo can also be manipulated by the amount of footage given a specific action and by the kind of buildup it receives in change of image size or angle. The final control of tempo is in the editing.[54]

Speed is accentuated by short shots, shots of great contrast.

In that sequence of Karen and Dean approaching each other from opposite directions, if you allow each shot to run long, their coming together seems a quite leisurely affair; if you have each shot brief, they seem to rush together.

Change of speed *within a sequence* can be manipulated through the general rule of changes in image size and angles.

A progression of image sizes from smaller to larger increases tempo—sharpens the sense of things happening faster. You'll find this is so whether the sequence is an unexciting budget conference in Mr. Producer's office or a tense episode in a Hollywood thriller where the would-be murderer closes in on the hero and the audience sees his strained face and upraised knife in successive, ever-larger closeups.

As far as angles are concerned, oblique angles and low angles when carefully used also quicken tempo. This holds true regardless of just what your story happens to be, whether it is the meeting of Trudy and Dean, or a parade, or a christening.

The tempo of a sequence *as a whole* cannot only be controlled by the length of each scene and the tempo *within* the scene, but also by the cut-ins and cut-aways used among the main shots.

Cut-ins usually heighten action more than cut-aways, since they are intimately connected with the main action rather than with a related one.

Again, length of cuts has a direct influence on the general tempo. A quick cut of horses' hooves, or shouting spectators at a race, conveys more speed and excitement than does a long one.

The nature of the subject likewise has a bearing on tempo. If you're shooting a sequence of a baby out for a ride in her carriage you'll find that a cut-in of the turning wheel conveys a stronger sense of motion than a CU cut-in of the child looking around—an action she might be performing from a statonary position.[55]

Control of tempo through continuity is obviously very strong. Never make the mistake, however, of putting the cart before the horse and trying to force slow or fast tempo on a subject, instead of letting the nature of the subject determine the tempo. You cannot, for example, have the same tempo in a basketball game as you would in a picnic story without getting a dull, disappointing film. But even in a swift basketball game, you *will* have intervals of slower action. The tempo for these slower-paced intervals should reflect the slowing down of the action. You can get your effect by using longer scenes of the players dribbling the ball or else by lengthening your cut-aways of spectators or substitutes and the coach watching the game.

Such a mixing of tempos is a great boon to your movie since it brings that wonderful quality of *variety* to it; a change of pace is as refreshing to your audience as a change of scene.

The meaning of tempo—and its application via pictorial continuity—is easy to grasp. There is no more esoteric mystery to it than there is to any of the other phases of motion picture technique, even though it may be somewhat more subtle. As with those other phases, you will gain skill and sureness through experience and careful attention.

A really great sense of timing is a rare gift; a movie man born with it has been endowed with a touch of genius. But fortunately for most of us non-geniuses, an adequate sense of timing can be developed by working at it.

When all is said and done, what counts in tempo is that the audience feels that the film *story* moves, that it progresses, keeps on unfolding at a suitable pace.[56]

COMPOSITION—"FRAMING" A SHOT

Your editorial judgment is also called on for good composition—*framing* a shot. The same esthetic factors that make a still picture pleasing to the eye are involved; but never allow yourself to forget that unlike the subject of a still picture, a motion picture subject is usually in motion. Unless you are shooting a travelogue, or a sequence in which the background has specific story value you want to bring out, your main concern in framing should be to keep your audience's attention on the *action,* to make it dominate other visual elements in the scene.

Keep the action fairly well centered on the screen, since the center is the natural focus of interest. That means you'll really have to be on your toes when panning action.

Framing closeups may require special care. That's because in some cameras, especially older models, the position of a CU in the viewfinder will not be identical with the position of the image in the lens; a CU centered in the viewfinder will be noticeably off-center in the lens. So to center the CU in the lens, it will be necessary to adjust the image off-center in the viewfinder.

However, you don't have to worry about parallax at all if your camera is equipped with a zoom lens with its own viewing tube or if you're using a reflex camera like the Arriflex.[57]

In framing action, take care not to cut off anything necessary to explain it. If you shoot a hockey game, don't frame the players from the knees up without ever showing their feet, since it is their ice skates which explains the fast-moving action.

You *can* hold off showing their feet until the sequence is well under way. This delay, if not protracted too long, is an excellent suspense—and surprise—device. That would be the effect should the audience, accustomed by TV to professional ice hockey, suddenly see a shot revealing the players are wearing roller skates.

Be sure in such a suspense surprise sequence to use a closeup to reveal the feet. The revelation is the climax of the sequence and should have attention concentrated on it by means of a CU. If you used a LS to disclose their method of locomotion, the action of the game would dominate the shot and weaken the punch of discovering the roller skates.

Shooting action closeups calls for special vigilance. Make the framing as *clean-cut* as possible, so that the meaning of each shot is clear. A CU of the roller skates should show them in their entirety, so that they are recognizable as roller skates, even if the swift action causes them to move in and out of the frame.

Careless framing of CUs becomes noticeable when the action is relatively slow or fixed in place, like a baby playing with a toy. A common failing of the beginning cameraman is to be so beguiled by baby's face that he fails to include the toy in the shot. The toy must be established clearly; after all, it is the key to the action. Once it is established, you can move in for tighter shots. Nor will it matter if the toy occasionally goes in and out of the frame as the baby plays with it.

This caution applies even more to framing ECUs, such as the baby's absorbed expression or the toy in its hand. These are highly desirable buildup shots, so don't hesitate to make them. Just take extra pains to avoid awkward or sloppy composition. In the ECU of the toy, try not to cut the baby's fingers in half; show their full length, or better yet, the entire hand. Try to show *a complete part.*

As for the ECU of the child's face, there is no objection to nipping off a bit of her head now and then with the top frame-line; just don't let it slip and slice her horribly through the eyes. If her head keeps bobbing up and down, pull back far enough with your camera so that the head does not move in and out of the frame repeatedly. It would be distressing to see her being scalped again and again.

FRAMING STATIC ACTION

Thus far you have been composing scenes of moving action, and your main concern has been to frame it fully and clearly so that audience attention is held consistently upon the motion.

Other composition considerations are minor as long as the screen shows plenty of movement with dramatic interest; the audience eye will be riveted upon it and oblivious of anything else. But you will inevitably have static scenes with virtually no movement by your subjects. In such cases, the conventional rules of composition—those that apply to a successful still picture or painting—can be helpful.

Compose your shot so that the audience eye will be led to see what you want it to see. Eliminate or reduce distracting elements. Make the scene as interesting, as eye-appealing as you can. Static does not mean dull.

Take pains to avoid visual monotony. When shooting static outdoor scenes that include the horizon, try to have the horizon line cross in the lower or upper third of the frame instead of in the middle, thereby splitting the frame into two equal parts. Keeping the horizon line in the lower third reduces foreground which is dead space when there is no action in it. Empty sky is preferable to empty earth.

When you can't help including a large stretch of unimportant foreground in the shot, try to use some element in it to catch and hold the audience eye; or else reduce the monotony of the foreground by breaking it up. You can use shadow to do this.

Suppose you are filming a long shot of worshippers entering a church on a hilltop, with much empty hillside in the foreground. Instead of resignedly shooting it that way, move around until your viewfinder frames the road winding up to the church and leading the eye right to it. Better still, wait until a car enters the frame and drives up on the road. With action in it, your foreground is no longer waste space. Even if your shot has to show the church alone, with no one going up the hillside, you can break up that monotonous foreground by scouting out some natural object like trees or rocks which throw a shadow.

You can use waste foreground to excellent advantage by manipulating the camera so that some object in the near foreground becomes *part of the frame line,* replacing the rigid line of the viewfinder. The doorway could serve to frame the LS of Mr. Producer's office. It may be seen, from this example, that a foreground object used for framing is not of great importance to the scene. It may be human or it may be inanimate. In either case, however, it serves the function of a prop which eliminates waste space and draws the eye to the main subject by creating contrast and a feeling of depth.

If you were shooting the aforementioned horse race, an excellent foreground frame could be found in a fence rail; a live prop could be found in the head and shoulders of a spectator. The human shape would not be in very sharp focus, but this would matter little since it would be recognizable in outline and would perform its framing function.

Framing can be done on the sides and background of your picture as well as the foreground. In that call on Mr. Producer, the sides of the office doorway could be used as a frame. Employing tree branches to frame the background at the top of a scenic shot is another familiar device. Framing material can be found most anywhere: a lamp will serve when shooting a living-room scene, a bush when shooting scenery.

As for a good background, it should—at the least—be free of anything that distracts the audience from the main subject. Don't have moving objects, such as a dog frisking around while you're shooting, your aunt spading her garden, or immobile objects whose size or shape are unusual enough to distract the viewer's eye from the main subjects. How often have you seen shots in which a background pole or tree seemed to be sprouting out of the head of the subject?

A good background, at best, will cause your subject to stand out more prominently by virtue of contrast. Never forget the graphic powers of light and dark, and the desirability of setting off your subject against a background of contrasting tone. A blonde will stand out much more effectively than a brunette against the dark of a shadowed doorway; equally, the brunette will photograph better against the white-painted wall of a house. The audience eye, by the way, is attracted to light tones before dark tones.

We have here given a resume of the important considerations of composition in framing shots.[58] We are frankly reluctant to dwell on the subject, because composition comes more and more into its own as action becomes increasingly static—in effect, less and less of a motion picture. It comes most fully into its own when shooting scenery, which is where the motion picture comes closest to the still picture. Motion picture cameramen who become entranced by static composition possibilities sometimes forget the importance of action.

WHEN THE SHOOTING IS OVER: EDITING FILM

Editing is the assembly of your film in the order and length you want to tell your story most effectively; it is the final stage in the application of pictorial continuity. It's when you look at your footage from the viewpoint of editor that you can best evaluate your work as cameraman. Now comes the moment of truth: Will that assortment of shots that seemed so great when you made them join together smoothly to tell a movie story?

Theoretically, final editing can be dispensed with when you have ideal shooting conditions: complete control and a detailed script. In such cases you can shoot your scenes with such precision that virtually no editing will be necessary afterward. In effect, this is known as *cutting in the camera.*

Cutting in the camera, like any state of perfection, can never be more than partly realized. Even in Hollywood, where shooting conditions come nearest to perfect control, there is a colossal amount of waste footage. Despite minutest care in advance planning, and the most costly preparations, the job of editing a Hollywood film after it is completed is almost as big as the job of shooting it.

In actual truth you—the non-professional—can come closer than Hollywood to cutting in the camera, because your picture plan is likely to be far more simple. But you too will inevitably have to do some final editing.

Film with mechanical faults such as edge fog or videotape with picture breakup, scenes in which the subject gawked into the camera, scenes that were reshot because a better angle was found—all will have to come out.

Such deletions are obvious musts. What is most important about final editing, what indeed makes it almost *mandatory,* is that you have an opportunity to look at your movie story the way the audience will see it. You get an exclusive preview, you have a chance to see how close you came to achieving the objective you were shooting for, you have the opportunity to rearrange scenes for smoother continuity or stronger dramatic effect, eliminate awkward continuity situations like jump cuts or other poor footage, to place your inserts, match action through overlap, make sure of correct screen direction, tinker with tempo and buildup, or even decide to reshoot some scenes. In short, you can polish your work as near to perfection as possible.

If you have taken a considerable number of shots, editing gives you a chance to put them in their proper order. Recall how, in those example sequences when shooting uncontrolled action that was moving fast—the horse race, the fire—you grabbed the most exciting shots first before they were no longer available, then took the buildup shots with greater leisure and care. Their being jumbled up in the camera didn't matter; you knew you could arrange them for continuity in the final editing.

There will be many times when you will finish shooting one movie story on the beginning of a roll of film, and start shooting another on the same roll. There will be times when you take various shots or sequences at random, to use in a more elaborate, fully planned movie story later on. In all such cases, the non-related shots will have to be cut out and filed separately.

Still another reason for final editing is the fact that it is wise, when shooting, to make your scenes a little long. The cautious cameraman will start his camera rolling just before his action begins and keep shooting for an instant after the action ends. You should not only make sure of getting the complete picture, but have additional frames for overlap or any other splicing contingencies. Always bear in mind the continuity truism that one cannot put into film while editing what was not registered on film when shooting.

As for tempo, editing gives you a shining opportunity to put into your picture more snap and speed where called for, or to pace it at a more tranquil rate of movement when that is appropriate. This, as we have seen earlier, is controlled by the length to which you trim your scenes and by the use you make of cut-ins and cut-aways. Remember that there isn't too much danger of making your shots too short when editing for tempo. It is a far more common fault for movies to drag than to move too briskly.

All too frequently, good tempo also demands the elimination of entire scenes or even sequences. They may be well shot and beautiful to look at, but they throw off the pacing of your story, or make it unnecessarily complicated, or they are simply *superfluous.* It may give you heartburn to throw out beautiful footage, but it is discipline as well as skill that makes the motion picture craftsman. Superfluous footage is simply film fat. Be a weight watcher!

The idea of throwing away footage—even trims—tends to make the nonprofessional wince. It will reassure him to know that every experienced cameraman, whether professional or not, learns to count on a margin of waste. It is inevitable.

Far more film is left on Hollywood cutting-room floors than ever appears in the local movie theatre. The ratio of discarded to used footage may run as high as ten to one, often higher! Even TV newsmen who are chronically pressed for time usually shoot several hundred per cent more tape on film than is actually used. So the non-professional need not feel he is throwing his money away if the needs of good continuity require him to discard a modest percentage of his film.

So don't take it to heart when you edit out that superfluous footage. What may at first seem like wastefulness is actually conserving—conserving the quality of your motion picture.[59]

WHEN THE SHOOTING IS OVER: EDITING VIDEOTAPE

All the continuity truisms you've just read about editing film hold true for videotape. However, the physical process of editing videotape is entirely different from that of film. It calls for different equipment and a different method of execution. We're going to give you just a brief, barebones description of those differences, since the technical aspects of editing, whether film or videotape, is not our theme. Pictorial continuity is; and editing is one of the means to the end of achieving pictorial continuity. If you want to get into the fine points of videotape editing, there is a wide range of excellent technical literature on the subject, just at there is on film editing.

Even before beginning the editing process, the video cameraman has a unique advantage over his film counterpart. He can look at what he's shot im-

mediately, unlike the film cameraman who must wait for his footage to be pro-
cessed and printed and returned to him before he can see how his shots turned
out. If his video camera has an electronic viewfinder, the video cameraman can
replay the tape right in the camera. He can't do this if the viewfinder is of the
optical kind, but then he can run his tape through his TV set at home; and
that's the next best thing to instant replay!

Another impressive feature of videotape is that it's reusable. So if you
don't like what you see when you play back what you've shot, you can *reshoot*
any or all of it right away on the same videtape, while you're still on the scene
and, hopefully, can command the same action.

This feature of reusability makes it easier for you to *cut in the camera*
when you reshoot. Just remember that every time you reuse the tape, you will
have some degradation of picture quality.

The odds are, however, that no matter how well you succeed at cutting in
the camera, there will still be awkward or irrelevant bits of footage you will want
to omit because they make your camera work look bad or because they inter-
rupt the story flow. Also, there will be scenes you'll want to drop as unnecessary and other scenes you will want to move around for better continuity
or dramatic effect. So you'll have to get into the editing process if you want a
good-looking, continuity-smooth movie story.

Now, how about the physical aspects of videotape editing? To begin with,
the fact is videotape is *never* cut and spliced physically the way film is. A
spliced tape run through a VCR (videocassette recorder) could cause serious
damage to the recording head. Instead, a copy is made by playing back the
original tape that was shot—or, in video language, "recorded" or "laid
down"—in the field.[60] The procedure can be compared to making a copy of
various segments of an audio tape. It is the new videotape that will hold the
scenes you select or assemble for your final edited "master." This primary
method of editing videotape is called the "assemble mode."[61]

In the assemble mode, the re-recorded scenes are laid down in any order
you wish in order to tell your story effectively with proper continuity.[62] If you've
shot your story in perfect continuity, with cut-aways and inserts in their proper
places and in the lengths you want, no editing—except to eliminate breakup—
is necessary since you will have an exact copy of the field tape.

However, if your original scenes are not in the continuity you want, you
can deviate from the order in which they were shot when you lay down your
new tape; that is, you can re-record Scene 1, then Scene 5, go back to Scene
2, then Scene 4, go back to 3, and so on. Keep in mind that every time you
deviate from the order in which the original scenes were shot, you will have an
edit.

You can also trim an overlong original scene by choosing a precise point
after the beginning and/or before the end of the scene and making your copy

between the two points. Here, too, you have an edit.

The same is true if you want to change a scene after the edited master is completed. The new scene you insert ("insert mode") must be the exact same length of the scene it replaces (otherwise you will have to redo the rest of the dubbed tape). Again an edit.

Professionally, these edits are made with electronic editing controllers in order to get clean edits free of picture breakup or similar electronic glitches.

It is true you can make an edited copy by a lashup of your neighbor's VCR with your own as long as they are compatible in tape size, plus two home receivers and appropriate connecting cable. We admire such enterprise and we certainly want the home video cameraman to edit his own footage. (More on that in the pages that follow.) However, without electronic editing equipment you will get picture breakup at the beginning of each edit. It is inescapable.

Now there are people who will say, so what? The home cameraman is not a professional shooting a commercial production; he's just shooting a little movie for himself, his family and friends. And what's a little picture breakup between friends?

Not in our book. We ask the non-professional, no matter what and why he shoots, to strive for professional standards not only for his personal gratification but for the sake of his audience, which is supposed to enjoy his movie story. That means making clean edits free of distracting and annoying picture breakup. For which electronic editing equipment is mandatory.

The problem is that electronic editing equipment is expensive. In the case of commercial broadcast equipment using ¾-inch, 1-inch or 2-inch tape widths, it is notoriously costly, with prices currently as high as six figures.

Even in the case of ½-inch videotape, a very popular size in home video cameras and which also has widespread commercial/industrial, non-broadcast use, buying an electronic edit controller at present can mean spending thousands of dollars. At the same "at present," there is no electronic editing equipment available for the smaller tape sizes of ¼-inch and 8mm utilized in smaller home video cameras that have come on the market.

This certainly puts the home cameraman who cannot afford today's prices for electronic editing equipment in a bind; the authors, too, for urging clean edits possible only with electronic editing equipment. However, terms like "today" and "at present" are highly transient in the world of video technology which continues to advance at astonishing speed. We don't think we are sticking our necks out by asserting that it is just a matter of time—and we mean a short time—that electronic edit systems will be available in all sizes used by the non-professional; and that initial high prices will drop rapidly just as they have for video cameras and tabletop VCRs; and so come within the buying range of any home or student cameraman. Speed the day!

DO YOUR OWN EDITING!

We're always surprised when we come across non-professionals who shy away from doing their own editing. This is true of beginners especially (and some professional cameramen). The excuses offered are varied: they haven't the time or lack the equipment because of cost; or feel they require technical knowledge; or prefer to have their footage edited "outside" because they believe their work will come out looking better; or simply, because they believe editing is a chore.

Few of these excuses hold up. You can't care very much about your work if you say you can't find the time to edit it. How else can you make sure your footage is seen to best advantage? How else achieve your goal of telling a good movie story, with proper pictorial continuity?

As to cost, film editing equipment for the beginner using 8mm or Super 8 is simply not expensive. If you fancy the more professional 16mm (or even 35mm) size, you can rent the equipment if buying it is too costly. Yes, the cost of videotape editing equipment is still a factor for the video cameraman who uses the popular ½-inch size, but rental equipment is available, too.

Regarding technical knowledge, for most non-professional purposes, such as a home movie or student exercise, it isn't any more difficult to learn the basics of film viewer, splicer and shears than it is to load a camera and set exposure and focus. True, operating electronic editing equipment even for ½-inch videotape is not quite that simple. On the other hand, it does not require profound expertise. It is readily grasped by anyone who sets his or her mind on learning the technique.

We can understand a beginning cameraman going to a professional to edit his footage (and paying the price) if he feels his own efforts at editing may be crude or sloppy. But like developing any skill, you're not going to get good at editing unless you work at it. This "hands on" experience-learning by doing—is an absolute must for the amateur who aspires to become a professional. To learn your craft, you have to practice it yourself, no matter how much help you get from a teacher or a textbook.

As for editing being a chore, that's unbelievable. It is one of the joys of moviemaking to see your work on film or videotape take shape under your hands, the shape that *you* want, not somebody else. We find it hard to accept the idea that anyone who planned and shot a movie story even on the simplest home movie theme; who worked on it not only as cameraman but also as his own producer, director, lighting man, utility man, etc., could bear the thought of a total stranger doing the editing. Allowing such a thing to happen to your brain child is like bringing a flesh-and-blood baby into the world and turning it over to someone else to be raised!

Okay, it's true that very few "big name" moviemakers do their own editing in the hands-on sense, whether it's a Hollywood film feature or a television network documentary. However, these people spend almost as much time on the editing process as the editor does, supervising and guiding the editor so that the finished work has a distinctly personal touch. So, if for any reason you do take your footage to a professional editor, tell him what you want and see that he does it. (Don't let yourself be intimidated by his greater experience; after all you're paying for his services!) That way you'll have creative control of the editing even if the hands-on work is done by a hired hand.

CAMERAMEN, THINK LIKE AN EDITOR!

A small word of caution: it's impossible to do a good job of editing unless your footage is *complete,* with all the variety of shots needed for pictorial continuity.

So when you go to shoot, think like an editor! A good cameraman tries to visualize the footage he's shooting as it will appear onscreen after the editor has done his work. So he shoots to give the editor everything he needs.

Even the veteran professional—a cameraman or the director guiding him—sometimes falls down in this respect. He forgets to shoot those all-important secondary shots—especially cut-aways—after the main action has been put on film or videotape.

This lapse, when committed by a news or documentary cameraman working under the pressures of time or uncontrolled action, may be understandable and—maybe—reluctantly condoned by his superiors. It is unforgivable when there is no time bind or the action was easily controlled.

SUMMARY

Pictorial continuity has a strong influence on the form and internal structure of a motion-picture story.

* This influence is expressed through the editorial judgment of the cameraman.
* Editorial judgment is exercised before shooting by means of *advance planning.*
* *Some* advance planning is desirable, whether it is a detailed scenario or a few mental notes.
* Editorial judgment exercised *during* shooting stamps the cameraman's individuality on each scene.
* Tempo determines the speed at which the story seems to move; it is affected by lengths of shots, rate of movement of action, use of cut-ins and cut-aways.
* The primary consideration of good composition in a motion picture is to focus attention on the main action, and to eliminate or reduce distracting elements.

• The final expression of editorial judgment is in the editing process: in placing cut-ins, cut-aways and other shots in their proper order, in matching action, in eliminating bad footage, in adjusting tempo, in creating good continuity to achieve the best possible movie story.

• All superfluous footage should be eliminated during the editing process. Even well-shot, photogenic scenes have a negative effect if they complicate the story or throw off its tempo. Superfluous footage is movie fat; get rid of it!

• The moviemaker should count on a sizeable percentage of his footage being eliminated during editing. This is unavoidable in striving for good pictorial continuity so it should not be regretted as waste.

• Shooting videotape is an electronic operation; so is its editing process.

• Editing videotapes is an entirely different process from editing film, but the objective is the same—to achieve good pictorial continuity.

• Electronic editing equipment is necessary in order to get "clean" videotape edits, free of picture breakup.

• Edit your own film. If you think equipment is too costly to buy, rent it. Don't turn over your footage to a professional film editor because you have doubts about your editing technique or your ability to achieve pictorial continuity. Learn by doing.

• Editing is not a chore. It is part of the fun of moviemaking to see your story take shape under your own hands.

• If you do take your footage to a professional editor, don't give him free rein; have him put together your story the way you want it.

• A good cameraman thinks like an editor, anticipating the need for the variety of shots needed for good pictorial continuity.

CHAPTER 14

THE ECONOMY OF CONTINUITY

LESS IS MORE

By now, we can appreciate how closely knit all the aspects of continuity are; how this advanced chapter is intimately related to the elementary one about the basic shots of the sequence, and both to the chapters inbetween; how a single shot should be considered—*at one and the same time*—in terms of all the various factors of continuity. The whole of continuity is, indeed, equal to the sum of its parts.

The reader, however, may sigh at the abundance and variety of things the full use of continuity requires—the special shots to take, the cut-ins and cut-aways, the things to watch out for: screen direction, clean exits and entrances, and so on. All to make a simple home movie.

You may be convinced of your ability to handle continuity from the viewpoint of ideas or technique, but you may at the same time wonder whether you have enough film or videotape for all the various continuity touches. "Doesn't it require far more footage," you may ask, "than if I just aimed the camera from one or two positions and banged away, getting everything in with one or two shots?"

The answer is unequivocally "No!" The shots made by the average beginner or student are individually much too long. He will start his camera from one position and simply let it run on far longer than necessary to get that one scene over to the audience. The unnecessarily exposed footage in any one of these overlong shots would easily be enough for several different scenes, along with cut-ins and cut-aways and other refinements of pictorial continuity.

Let's look at some figures by way of illustration. We'll use Super 8, the most popular film size among amateurs today; then give you the equivalent figures in 16mm, a size widely favored by professional moviemakers for documentaries, educational, and industrial use.

A Super 8 cameraman unfamiliar with the uses of good continuity might expose as much as ten feet (18 feet in 16mm) for a single shot from the same position. Example: a sequence showing the family gathered around Junior's birthday cake. The cameraman explains that he let the camera run on because "I can get almost everybody in from this spot and since there are quite a few people in the scene, I want the shot to run long enough so that the audience has a chance to see everyone!"

Then—since a few people were left out—he moves his camera to an angle from which he can get them "into the picture" too and makes another shot as long as the first, if not longer. By now he has exposed twenty feet or more of Super 8 (36 feet in 16mm)—very dull stuff, needless to say.

How much better his movie would be if, with his first ten feet, he shoots a real sequence! Let's say about three-and-a third feet on a LS, three feet on a MS, a CU of Junior cutting the cake for another two-and-a-third feet, with a one-and-a-third foot insert of the knife as it plunges through the frosting (the equivalent, *roughly,* in 16mm would be: LS, 6 feet; MS, 5 feet; CU, 4 feet; insert, 3 feet).

With the remaining unexposed footage, he can still "get everybody in"—and make the film far livelier—if he takes a reestablishing shot of about three feet in Super 8 that shows Junior handing out slices of cake, then several closeups one or two feet long showing the guests blissfully gorging themselves. He ends with a final LS—using whatever film remains—of Junior looking ruefully at the empty cake plate as he scoops up the crumbs.[63] (You can figure out the lengths in 16mm if you use a ratio of approximately 9 to 5 in Super 8.)

No doubt you've noticed that we didn't give you lengths of footage in videotape. It is an idiosyncrasy of video that the amount of footage recorded is figured in minutes and seconds of running time, not in feet or inches, whereas film is figured both ways. The running time for the twenty feet of Super 8 and the thirty-six feet of 16mm is about 60 seconds. The equivalent running time for videotape is approximately the same.

The ultimate truth about applying continuity to a movie is this: not only does it require *no more* than the ordinary amount of footage, but it actually leads to more economical usage! The unplanned, blind act of just shooting a roll of film or tape cassette at random changes to a careful appraisal of scene lengths to achieve maximum effectiveness in telling your story.

NOT JUST DOLLARS AND CENTS

We do not emphasize the economy of continuity merely out of concern for cost. If expense alone were the factor, the award would go to videotape. Its purchase price is higher than film, but you get far, far more running time in a video cassette than you do in a film roll, regardless of size. You also get the advantage of reusability. (Regarding the expression "running time," it's a peculiarity of video that the amount of videotape that is shot is expressed in minutes and seconds; whereas the amount of film shot is usually expressed in feet.)

Now, when we talk economy, we also lay stress on getting the most efficient results from the footage, film or videotape, that you have on hand for your "shoot." We not only want to see you reduce waste, we want to see you get the most out of the time and effort you put into shooting your story.

YOU CAN'T ARGUE
WITH ARITHMETIC

The economy of continuity is so great we're going to give you another example, which should be conclusive.

Let's say you're a student cameraman. Your instructor has given you a shooting assignment. It's about a workman shoveling sand onto a truck. You're under orders to make it brief, to cut in the camera as much as possible. This gives you some concern since the action is uncontrolled. You're afraid you may have to shoot a lot of footage that will never make it to the final, edited version—in a word, waste.

Not so! Take note of the following arithmetic. Again we'll use figures in Super 8. It's possible that as a student you'll be given a 16mm camera to shoot with. In that case, we'll leave it to you to transpose the Super 8 figures into 16. Use the formula we gave you in the preceding sequence.

First you put the establishing shot to work and make a LS of the man as he attacks the sandpile with his shovel. You shoot three-and-a-third feet, a full ten seconds, to establish the action. Another three feet will take care of your MS and CU. The overall action is simple and repetitious; if you stay on it too long from the same angle it becomes monotonous.

Now get going on your cut-ins and cut-aways for buildup. You shoot a full-frame cut-in, a CU, of the shovel as it digs into the sandpile and withdraws with its load out of the frame, comes back empty, is refilled, and goes out of the frame again. Two feet for this shot. Add a CU of the workman's face and one of his hands gripping the shovel for more buildup. Again, two feet.

You change your angle completely but stay in close, almost filling your frame with the shovel. You shoot two more shovelfuls being removed. Two feet more. If the workman's face is particularly interesting because of character lines or other facial features, shoot another CU for buildup. Two feet. Do not drag out an interesting subject with excessive footage!

For a fresh approach to the action, you change your angle again. This time you frame the view against the sky, with the edge of the truck just inside the frame. You shoot the shovel coming into the frame fully loaded with sand and watch the sand leave the shovel and fall into the truck. You keep the camera motionless while the action is repeated. (The empty frame between shovelfuls creates a slight pause which is buildup in itself). To allow the shovel enough time to go to and from the sandpile, let the shot run about three-and-a-third feet. Switch your camera position again for a really low-angle shot looking up into the perspiring face of the man shoveling. One-and-a-third feet are enough.

At this point you give the camera and yourself a rest. You sit down and wait until the truck is about half full. Now's a good time to answer a question on your mind. Where are the cut-aways? Answer: what you see is what you get—on film or tape. If there's nothing suitable as a cut-away (a spectator, for instance), there's nothing to shoot. Wouldn't it be neat if a little child came along with a toy shovel and stopped to watch the workman? But no child, no spectator, no cut-away.

The truck is about half full, so pick up your camera again. Find yourself a position for a nice high-angle shot. From this new vantage point, shoot a re-establishing shot of the sand in the truck; then go past it to the man in the background working on the remainder of the sandpile. Three feet.

Take another break until the workman has only about three shovelfuls of sand left; then return to your original position and shoot him as he dumps the final loads aboard the truck and mops his brow. Three feet will cover this action.

So far you have shot twenty-five feet of Super 8. Your action is complete but to add a satisfying finishing touch you move across the street for a final LS showing the workman as he climbs aboard the truck and drives out of the frame. Three feet should do it for this closing scene.

The total now is 28 feet, give or take a fraction or so. When you edit this material and trim some of the longer shots (for the chances are far greater that you shot too much rather than too little), you will find that your finished sequence is reduced to about twenty-five or twenty-six feet. Running time would be in the neighborhood of a minute and a quarter or so.

Thus the action of sand removal, an operation that took at least a half-hour, is run through on the screen in well less than two minutes—clearly, convincingly, *interestingly,* with no part of the story left untold and with extreme economy of footage.

So, in answer to the question of whether you will need a lot of footage to apply pictorial continuity every time you shoot, the answer is, most emphatically, no!

DON'T GO OVERBOARD

There is a tendency among many a freshman cameraman—whether he is a college youth or a family adult—to go overboard while shooting regardless of whether or not he is concerned about cost. We are not referring to the beginner who takes an overlong shot from one camera position; but to the novice movie maker who keeps re-shooting the same scene "to get the action a little better" or to see how many different photographic angles he can get.

If he is reminded that *only one* of these many similar shots can be used in the final, edited movie, he will shrug off his overshooting by saying that film or videotape is the cheapest part of movie making and he doesn't want to risk undershooting to save a few cents or a few minutes.

Now it is true that a professional cameraman will shoot as much as he needs to properly cover his story and give his editor a generous choice of insert shots. False economy could be disastrous.

But there is a difference between the sort of ample coverage by which a cameraman protects his story—and himself!—and footage shot out of sheer exuberance without regard to story needs or pictorial continuity.

Sure it's the cameraman's privilege to squander his footage (and time) as he sees fit, as long as he doesn't try to kid himself or anyone else that it serves any purpose toward shooting a movie story properly.

As for the aspiring movie maker who wants to keep costs down but tends to shoot an excess of footage because he is unsure of his needs, he'll find that following the rules of pictorial continuity intelligently, will avoid unnecessary overshooting. Pictorial continuity imposes a structured form on a story, prescribes the kinds of shots needed, and implies their comparative length. It gives the beginner clear-cut guide lines which, if followed, will conserve without constricting his pictorial imagination or creativity.

HOW ABOUT STORY MATERIAL?

Another question that may be on your mind is: Do simple domestic picture subjects lend themselves to all these varied touches of good continuity?

The answer can easily be inferred from the illustrations we have used throughout; they have been drawn consistently from the personal environment and the daily affairs of almost any home movie maker.

There is no aspect of home life too small or too static to be built up into some kind of story. That is one of the great services of continuity—to take a subject which at first glance seems to offer opportunity for no more than a still-camera shot and build it up into a genuine motion picture story,

Any subject taken at random will lend itself to this treatment. Here, let's pick on you, the reader. What are you doing at this moment?: reading this book. That might make a nice still shot. But it will do more, it will make a motion picture.

Surprising? Well, it can be done by applying the resources of pictorial continuity. Here's how it might break down into a motion picture sequence.

1. LS of living room with copy of this book on end-table next to easy chair. A few feet of this—then you, the reader, make clean entrance, walk over to chair, sit down.

2. MS from change of angle. Camera is moved in front of chair near floor and angled up at you as you stretch out, look down at table, see book.

3. CU from side angle near end-table with book in foreground as you stretch out hand, pick it up, look at it.

4. ECU cut-in, from over your shoulder, of book to show title.

5. CU of your face as you study title.

6. LS to reestablish as you look up at clock on mantel over fireplace, then look down to book and begin to read.

7. CU cut-away to clock to show hands at one o'clock, then dissolve into . . .

8. . . . CU from another angle on clock showing time at three o'clock.

9. MS of you reading page near end of book.

10. MS from another angle as you close book, lay it on table.

11. LS from corner of room opposite to doorway as you rise, with camera panning you over to doorway. Out you go through doorway and out of the frame.

The sequence is finished in about the same amount of footage used in the sand-shoveling story. A movie has been made out of a subject that at first glance seemed completely static and impossible of development as a motion picture story.

But this is only scratching the surface of what can be done to build up the ordinary, everyday subject of reading a book. A sequence of you lighting a cigarette (not that we endorse smoking) could be cut in, followed by a dissolve from a shot of one cigarette stub in the ashtray to a shot of a trayful of butts indicating the passage of time.

Still more meat could be added by a third sequence showing you putting the book face down when you reach the chapter on panning, getting out your camera, and practicing a pan. (This sequence, indeed, could very well be divided into two or more subordinate sequences.)

The movie could be given a comic twist by having Junior run back and forth with his toys, or chase the dog. Such a sequence would provide plenty of opportunity to apply the new knowledge of panning and directional continuity, with head-ons and tail-aways of Junior, cut-ins of his racing feet, cut-aways of the dog, and the like. Things could be worked up to a furious tempo by brief flashes of Junior dashing to and fro and quick shots inbetween of your harried, exasperated expression.

Finally to put a good ending on the whole picture, there could be a sequence of you grabbing the book and your camera, clapping your hand on Junior's shoulder, pointing outdoors, and marching him off with the obvious intention of practicing a little of what you have been reading . . . so on out of the room in a nice fade-out.

Any subject at all is susceptible to treatment by pictorial continuity; conversely, pictorial continuity will build up a genuine motion picture out of any subject.

SUMMARY

There is economy in good continuity. We mean economy not only in terms of cost, but also in the most effective use of the cameraman's time and effort.

* Indiscriminate over-shooting is self-indulgence by the cameraman; it is never justified by the requirements of good continuity. And it is expensive.

* The moviemaker who tends to overshoot because he is unsure of himself, will find that the disciplined approach to shooting demanded by pictorial continuity will give him all the shots he needs without wastefulness.

* He needn't worry whether simple subjects like family events lend themselves to continuity treatment. They most emphatically do; pictorial continuity will build a genuine motion picture out of any subject.

CHAPTER 15

THINK MOTION PICTURES!

THE GHOST OF STILL-PICTURE PSYCHOLOGY

The use of pictorial continuity is the secret of *good* moviemaking. It is the easiest, simplest, most economical way because it is the correct way. But—and this is something to be thankful for—even the most expensive, gadget-studded camera hasn't got pictorial continuity built into it. The cameraman must learn to think in terms of pictorial continuity. And this means simply that he must *think motion pictures.*

But it isn't something that just comes naturally. It's not hard, but there is an obstacle to overcome. Most moviemakers—just about all of us, really—took still pictures before we picked up a movie camera. Unfortunately, the ghost of still-picture psychology keeps on hovering around many a beginning motion picture cameraman. He continues to *think* as a still photographer, especially if he was a good one!

He finds it hard to assimilate the idea that the motion picture story calls for a much different technique than still pictures and therefore a vastly different approach in his thinking.

Motion pictures mean what they say—*motion*! This is so obvious a truism that many a novice film maker resents being reminded of it, especially when he claims to understand and accept the difference between stills and movies. He remains unaware that when shooting a movie story, he may still—unconsciously—be applying still picture psychology.

Operating a film or video camera with still camera technique will get you pictures all right; if you are a competent still photographer, the pictures no doubt will be good in the sense of being well exposed, nice and sharp, probably well composed, even lively. And these qualities are important in giving your movies visual appeal.

But without pictorial continuity, they will not be motion pictures. They will be animated still pictures. Perhaps you will be content to have them so. But we think it an awful shame if you ask of your motion picture camera only what any decent still camera will give you—a good, sharp, pleasing likeness.

You will also be unfair to the ability of the motion picture camera to do more than just render a likeness; you will be ignoring its unique ability to tell a living story.

You will also be unfair to yourself, because the apparent trouble of breaking down action into sequences, and sequences into separate shots, the "bother" of observing pictorial continuity, are really no problems at all, but add immeasurably to the sheer fun of moviemaking. Once you try it, the involvement in getting buildup shots, of establishing tempo, and so on, will warm you up, exhilarate you with an appeal to your imagination and your creative instinct—an instinct that is latent in every camera buff.

Look at the question from the viewpoint of your prospective audience. Every movie fan who has seen good and bad movies is sensitive to continuity. He may not be consciously aware of it—he may never even have heard of the term—but it has had its influence on him just the same.

He takes it for granted when he sees a good motion picture; he knows it is moving smoothly from scene to scene, sequence to sequence, climax to climax.

If the picture, however, moves jerkily, without coherence or flow—*if continuity is lacking*—the moviegoer feels its absence even though he cannot say in so many words what is lacking. Your audience, your family and friends, and you will miss it just as much in your movies, even if they're modest ones for home consumption.

The cause is the same—and the remedy is the same. You do not use watercolor technique when painting a canvas in oils; it is as illogical to handle a motion picture camera as though it were a still camera. You cannot have a true motion picture, without pictorial continuity.

So kiss the ghost of still-picture psychology goodbye. Think, feel and shoot as a motion picture cameraman![64]

A SOFT WORD TO THE
YOUNG MOVIE MAKER

There are often trends and fashions in motion picture making just as there are in other story telling media, such as the novel or the play. Some of these trends and fashions are creative, so they remain and enrich the medium; others, being fads, die out after their novelty has faded.

One of the fashions that seems to recur, especially among younger movie makers, is to subordinate plot to mood; to arouse feeling only through visual imagery, rather than by way of a strong narrative with sharply defined characters.[65]

It is not within the realm of this book to discuss the esthetic pros and cons of this fashion. We wish only to point out that to be effective, this type of movie is critically dependent on good continuity. Any flaw, any lapse in pictorial continuity, will create a visual jar that will break the mood; its de-emphasis of dialogue requires the film to be rich in buildup and smooth in transitions.

There are some extremists who reject any kind of discipline or structure in movies as hindering their "creative freedom"; they disdain technique as "nuts and bolts," blocking the spontaneity and free flow of artistic expression. We can only answer that if they do not apply pictorial continuity to their movie making, they will not end up with a motion picture. They will have a series of visual images, but without the connective tissue of pictorial continuity, they will have created a "non-movie."

We hasten to add that we are all for spontaneity and creativity. Throughout this text we have stressed the flexibility of pictorial continuity. We affirm that there is nothing sacred or unchangeable about its rules. Experimentation and change are refreshing; the visual medium can always profit by bold new ideas that enrich its visual impact and enlarge its power to communicate. It is always possible that revolutionary changes may appear in the art of movie making.

So far, however, nothing of the kind has happened. True, there have been sweeping changes in subject matter, taste and treatment; there have been remarkable improvements in equipment. And of course video has given us an entirely new medium. Yet the basic technique of today—despite some flashy innovations—still rests on the work of the early master, David Wark Griffith. And Griffith was not a revolutionary, he was a developer; he took the crude techniques of motion picture's infant days and brought them to maturity. The many great moviemakers that followed him—in America, Europe and the Far East—simply sharpened and polished his techniques with enormous skill and creativity.

No movie genius comparable to the great revolutionaries in the other arts has appeared as yet; we have no cinematic da Vincis, Picassos,or Stravinskys. But then the other arts existed for thousands of years before their innovative giants emerged; the art of the motion picture is not even a century old!

Perhaps you may be the one to blaze new trails in moviemaking; create boldly original, radically new approaches to the art. More power to you! But please bear one thought in mind: the great revolutionaries in the other arts were all master craftsmen who knew their medium exhaustively; the memorable moviemakers of yesterday and today were, and are, superb technicians who travelled the long road of experience before they achieved their enduring works of imagination and skill.

We sum up our word to young moviemakers: Be fair to your talent, be fair to your ambition, be fair to your creativity—*learn your craft first.*

FADE-OUT

You cannot have a good motion picture without pictorial continuity. That is our final word.

That is why we have taken pictorial continuity as the major subject of this book and have emphasized repeatedly—*ad nauseam,* no doubt—that it applies equally and fully to video as well as film, since video is just as much a medium for motion pictures. Dialogue, music, sound effects, these are familiar adjuncts of the movie of today, but they are grafted on, they are not *inherent motion picture qualities.* They are aural, not visual qualities. A motion picture with good continuity can be enhanced by them; but if its continuity is bad or non-existent, aural embellishments are like so much baling wire, desperately—and obviously—used to keep the picture from falling apart. So in this book we have put first things first, and have occupied ourselves basically, with continuity.[66]

The innate quality of pictorial continuity in a good motion picture is also the reason we have addressed this book not only to anyone who wants to shoot better movies or who has ambitions for writing or directing them, but to the person who wants to *understand* them better as well, whether for his greater enjoyment as a spectator or because he is interested in the motion picture as an art form.

We believe the motion picture to be the greatest medium for story-telling; we believe it offers just as rich opportunities for expression as painting or literature. But we also believe it to be a unique medium with a special technique of its own, which must be understood.

So to all devotees of the motion picture—the family man who doesn't give a nickel for "art" content but wants to shoot a good home movie of baby, the young moviemaker who aspires to movies as a career, the professional critic or just the average moviegoer who has never loaded a camera but is interested in what a motion picture story can tell, we say: *Know your medium*—learn pictorial continuity—and enjoy it!

CHAPTER 16

A P.S. ON VIDEO

ONCE MORE WITH FEELING

There are people who, after going through this book, may sincerely wonder why there isn't more emphasis on video than on film; indeed, why it wasn't given precedence over film since video is the newer medium, a very exciting one and whose use is constantly increasing. As a matter of fact, video cameras are now outselling film cameras.

Well now, we don't believe video will replace film any more than its broadcast television version made radio obsolete. Film is alive and well, thriving, not only in Hollywood feature production but in industrial, educational and home use.

There are millions of film cameras (and other equipment like projectors) in service. They are sturdy reliable instruments which in some cases have been in use for decades and may well be around decades longer. Video cameras and other equipment are increasingly well made but because they are electronic in nature, they are more vulnerable to technical operating problems.

But the most important point of all is that this is not a book about cameras or the technical aspects of two great visual media. It is a book about how to shoot a *movie story* regardless of whether it's on film or videotape.

It's not science fiction to speculate that in this high-tech era, a brand-new medium for telling a motion picture story may be developed, something unprecedented in the way it produces the illusion of motion pictures, employing a new type of camera as radically different from film and video cameras as they are different from each other.

Nonetheless, the cameraman shooting with this new kind of camera will still have to apply the timeless technique of pictorial continuity if he wants to tell a movie story that will capture the attention of an audience and hold it.

And that, friends, is the bottom line.

Good shooting!

TRIMS AND OUT-TAKES

It was our hope that you would go through all of the text first and get a grasp of the complete range of pictorial continuity without interrupting your reading to look at footnotes. Now if you wish to check the footnotes after reading the text, we believe you'll find them more meaningful and informative. Their source in the text is easily located by the reference number, and the page number in the text.

The movie terms "trims" and "out-takes" in the chapter heading above are used as similes for these footnotes, so we'll define them first as a typical footnote entry.

Ref. No. Re: trims and out-takes, page 128

When trim is used as a verb in the editing process, it applies to both film and videotape and means shortening a scene by getting rid of superfluous footage. In film, this is done by literally cutting it away. The remnant that was cut away is called a trim. It is in its use as a noun that trim appears in the title of this chapter.

However, there is no such noun usage in video since there is no discarded remnant of videotape. You do not use scissors on videotape to remove superfluous footage, you simply do not re-record the excess.

As to out-take, since the word derives from take used as a noun, we'll define that first. A take in film is any exposed length of film of a particular action or scene. If the cameraman or director decides to reshoot it for whatever reason, the original take becomes Take 1, the second Take 2, and so on in numerical order if more takes are shot.

The moviemaker may decide to print just one of these takes before the film is sent in for processing; or he may have them all printed and make his choice after he sees what they look like.

An out-take refers to the printed takes that are put aside after the decision is made to use one particular take. The surplus takes are not discarded immediately; they are retained until the film is *locked up* or completed in case there is a change of mind. Even then, some or all of the out-takes may be kept permanently in a film library where they are referred to as *library* or *stock* footage.

Video uses these terms in pretty much the same way except that out-takes are not assembled together in a group; they are left on the original, recorded tape.

It was only natural that video adopted the vocabulary of film since its story-telling technique is the same. Of course it added terms of its own—like video and videotape.

While we're on semantics, please notice that throughout this book we do not use the term "cutter," which in film is synonymous with "editor." That's because of video; you do not physically cut videotape. So to avoid confusion, we use the term "editor" exclusively.

However, "cut" as a verb may turn up in expressions that a videotape editor as well as a film editor may use. He may describe shots that move smoothly from one to the next as shots which *cut together,* strictly a metaphor. Chances are he was a film editor before he was a videotape editor.

Also, consider the use of the word "cut" as a noun, meaning a scene or shot edited into—or out of—a sequence. For example, "Let's use (or drop) that cut of the suspect chewing his fingernails."

Then there is the familiar metaphor of "cutting in the camera" to roil the semantic waters. This expression has nothing to do with the physical act of cutting footage. It means shooting your shots in the order and length in which you want them to appear onscreen. Editing them mentally, as it were. The expression is used in connection with video as well as with film cameras.

CHAPTER 1

1. Re: establishing shot, not location shot, page 10

Note the use of the words "locale" (or "setting") instead of "location." This fussiness is to avoid encouraging you to use the term "location shot" as a synonym for "establishing shot," as some people do. Such usage is best avoided since not every location shot is an establishing shot of the action.

Use *location shot* in the sense of a shot away from the studio, in real daily life settings, but don't make the mistake of considering it as strictly an exterior shot. It can be an interior shot as well. If you're "on location" at a cattle ranch, a shot of a horse being shoed inside the stable is as much of a location shot as one of cattle being branded on the open range.

2. Re: establishing shot and master shot, page 10

Let's clarify the use of these two terms. They are often confused because they have a lot in common. You will find the term *establishing shot* used frequently throughout the text, but *master shot* not at all. There are reasons, but first let's differentiate between the two terms: an *establishing shot* identifies the scene and the participants in it at the beginning of the action. The rest of the action is then filmed in a succession of different shots at different angles. However, when *all* the action is shot from the *single* angle of the opening establishing shot, it is known as a *master shot.*

In professional productions in which the action is fully controlled, as on a stage set, complete sequences are first filmed as master shots. Then the sequence is *reshot* with a variety of angles. The master shot is valuable as a protection in editing the film. If the editor feels a closer angle he has is unsatisfactory for some reason, he can cut back to the master shot to maintain continuity.

Yes, a movie story can be told entirely in master shots, but it would be visually monotonous. As we pointed out at the very beginning of Chapter 2, the human eye wants to get closer to the subject it is looking at; and it does so through a variety of angles which we simulate with the camera. It is this rich variety of angles—used with creative selectivity—that give film and video their unique appeal and excitement. In Chapter 12, we describe the use of "buildup" shots as putting the frosting on the movie cake. A movie shot entirely in master scenes would give you the shell of the cake—and no filling!

So we have avoided asking the beginner cameraman to think in terms of master scenes. Let him first learn how to build a pictorial sequence and enrich it with a variety of additional shots.

P.S. A master scene has nothing to do with "master positive." This is a film lab term for a certain fine-grain raw stock used in the process of making duplicate prints. It has no connection with pictorial continuity.

3. Re: steady camera shots, page 11
Use a tripod. No hand-held shot can be as steady as one taken with a tripod. You won't always be able to, but whenever you are in full control of the action and aren't pressed for time—as in this situation with Mr. Producer—use a tripod. Shaky shots are hard on the eyes—and on your reputation as a cameraman.

Do not be influenced by the frequent appearance of shaky hand-held shots in so-called "cinema vérité" films. We are not knocking "cinema vérité" as a documentary style, but shaky hand-held shots do not contribute to realism; rather they have the opposite effect. Sloppy camera work *of any kind* is unprofessional and except for the raw beginner, inexcusable; except if you're shooting in the middle of a war, explosion, or earthquake!

4. Re: the medium shot and the zoom, page 12
Avoid zooming just for zooming's sake. There is no need for a zoom in this

simple sequence on Mr. Producer. Zooming to a medium shot would be visual overkill.

5. Re: a pictorial hazard in shooting CUs, page 13

All of us have seen exaggerated CUs in television and in films in which parts of the subject's head or chin are sliced off; and other features like nose, mouth and skin pores grossly enlarged. These distortions are not the way the human eye sees people; they make even the most attractive face look grotesque. So unless you're shooting specifically for a bizarre effect, don't go overboard!

6. Re: the close shot, page 14

A first cousin to the close shot is the *medium close shot.* Some purists may insist this means a shot in between medium and close, but nearer to close. That's okay but don't make a big thing of it. The student movie maker, perhaps because of insecurity, tends to get involved in the semantics of terminology. Remember—be flexible.

7. Re: the shots in a sequence, page 14

The kind of shots used in a sequence, and the order in which they are to be made, are sometimes referred to as a *shot pattern* or *shot layout.* A *shot list* is a kind of shopping list of shots to be obtained, not necessarily in the order in which they will appear in the final edit.

CHAPTER 2

8. Re: the ELS, page 20

When an ELS is used to establish the scenic or atmospheric background of a movie story, it is sometimes called a *location shot.* This is not an exclusive meaning. *Any* shot away from the studio is a location shot. (*See* footnote 1.)

9. Re: the ECU, page 20

You may also see the extreme closeup abbreviated as "XCU."

10. Re: the full-figure shot, page 21

When a subject fills the screen snugly, like the illustration of Grant's Tomb, the shot is also known as a *full screen shot;* or more simply, as a *full shot.*

Yes, a medium shot or a CU or ECU can also be referred to as a full shot when it is tightly framed. You've guessed it—a *tight shot* means the same thing.

A tight shot is a good springboard for discussing its opposite—the *wide shot,* which also means exactly what is says. However, it is *relative* to its subject matter. A wide shot could be a full shot of a group of persons, a medium shot of a truck, a long shot of a 747 jetliner, or a close shot with a wide angle lens of the front line of a parade. It wouldn't make much sense, though, to call for a wide shot of an infant in a high chair, a football or a coin!

CHAPTER 3

11. Re: the pull back, page 22

Keep in mind that the pull back as used here is *not* a moving shot in which the camera is shooting while it is in motion, as in a dolly shot. (*See* Chapter 9, Moving Shots.) As used here, pull back means that the camera is stopped after the CU is shot; then moved to another stationary position farther from the subject after which the camera is started again to shoot the reestablishing shot.

We make this distinction because pull back is also used to indicate a moving shot, especially among TV studio cameramen who may say "push in" and "pull back" for "dolly in" and "dolly out."

12. Re: the establishing shot, page 23

There are frequent variations of the rules of pictorial continuity. This holds true of the one about the reestablishing shot usually being a long or medium shot. Here's an example: After the secretary finishes taking dictation in the second sequence, the third sequence could open with a CU—or an ECU—of the secretary's hands typing. Then the camera would pull back to an MS or LS to show she has returned to her own office.

13. Re: the reverse angle, page 28

The reverse angle has other uses besides that of reestablishing. It is another continuity device for filming lengthy movement, whether a fast-moving chase sequence or a slow stroll along city streets.

It is also used to add visual variety to a static scene, such as a couple eating dinner at a restaurant table or a group of people playing cards.

CHAPTER 4

14. Re: jumpy action, page 29

This is usually referred to by anguished film editors as a *jump cut.*

15. Re: controlled and uncontrolled action, page 33

This situation would be made easier if at least one of the cameras is equipped with a zoom lens. This would be standard procedure if a TV news department sent out two cameramen to cover that four-alarm fire.

In this case, some professionals would prefer to have the camera with the ordinary lens shoot only long shots to cover the overall action (master scene) and use the camera with the zoom lens for MSs and CUs.

16. Re: video switching, page 33

In technical language it's because the cameras and the switcher all "reference" the same sync pulse, which usually originates in a sync pulse generator referred to as *house sync.*

CHAPTER 5

17. Re: cut-aways and reaction shots, page 37

Some cut-aways are also known as *reaction shots.* This would apply to Freddy watching Johnny and the dog, or townspeople witnessing the sheriff-gunslinger confrontation, or to a porter waiting for the actor to finish packing his bags. They are *involved* in the action, reacting to it, even though they may be only passive observers at this point.

On the other hand, a car driving past Johnny and the dog, a sign identifying the town where the shootout is about to happen or a luggage hand truck the porter has brought are all cut-aways but not reaction shots.

18. Re: head-on and tail-away shots, page 38

Incidentally, a tail-away used right after a head-on shot—or the other way around—is a reverse angle.

Some readers may wonder whether such exactness of definition is not simply nit-picking or semantic fussiness. Not so. Precision of terminology is important in communicating the visual concepts of pictorial continuity, especially in the group effort that professional moviemaking requires.

Note that each shot or continuity point is named according to its function. The vocabulary employed in shooting a movie story is as exact and specific as that of engineering or music; but it is far easier to understand since it is drawn from everyday language.

However, every living language undergoes changes; there are shifts in emphasis, use and interpretation. Even the precise language of movies is affected. Some moviemakers, particularly those involved in shooting documentaries for television, do not use the term "cut-in," preferring to call for a closeup of a particular action. They also avoid the broad term "insert" which covers both cut-ins and cut-aways. (Inserts are discussed on pages 38 and 39.)

On the other hand, the term "cut-away" is more widely used than ever; and is as much a part of basic terminology as the long shot, medium shot and closeup.

So there are terms explained in Trims and Out-Takes you may seldom see or hear even if you become deeply involved in moviemaking; but if you do see or hear them, you won't be caught short trying to understand them.

19. Re: video insert, page 38

The term *insert* has a special meaning in video. It's applied to a shot that replaces part of another shot so that both are seen at the same time. Example: a tennis match with a player's wife watching shown in an insert.

Insert mode is a different video term. It refers to a videotape-editing process described in Chapter 13.

20. Re: the normal lens, page 43

It is *normal* because it perceives pretty much the same image the naked eye does from the same position.

CHAPTER 6

21. Re: zoom lenses on other film cameras, page 44

The 8mm, Super 8, and 35mm cameras have similar zoom lenses that produce similar effects in changing the image size.

8mm cameras have zoom lenses that vary with the manufacturer such as 10mm to 30mm and 8mm to 64mm. Super 8 zoom lenses are about the same.

As for the 35mm camera, a common zoom lens has a ratio from 25mm to 250mm. This ratio can be increased with auxiliary attachments, producing a much longer lens.

CHAPTER 7

22. Re: effect of long- and wide-angle shots on head-on angles, page 49

The use of the long lens in a head-on shot will slow down those horses even more, making them seem to take forever before coming close to the camera. A wide-angle lens will make those horses seem to rush at the camera like thunderbolts!

A comment is inevitable here about the widely popular use of the long lens for shooting chase sequences in feature films.

The effect is to drastically slow down the movement of the pursuer or the pursued, whether on foot, horseback or in a car or other vehicle. It stretches out on the scene, creating the impression that neither the pursuer or pursued is gaining on the other.

It is, of course, an optical illusion, a camera trick. But don't jump to the conclusion that we condemn it out of hand, any more than we did unusual angles. Long lens chase shots can be visually arresting; they can create drama and suspense.

The danger is that the drama and suspense can turn to tedium by overuse of the long lens shot; just as its visually arresting quality will self-destruct if audience attention is made to shift from the illusion—to how the illusion is made.

How long should you run such a shot; how often should you use it? We cannot tell you. The answer lies with you—in your taste, judgment and restraint as applied to the context of your film. We could say that when in doubt, don't use it, but we really don't believe the beginner cameraman is going to deny himself a chance to play around with what we ourselves describe as a widely popular shot.

But once you get the impulse to play or experiment out of your system, and settle down to shooting a movie story as professionally as you can, remember that what is a widely popular shot may be wildly overused, making it a bore. And that you don't want!

CHAPTER 8

23. Re: the use of "pan up" and "pan down" for "tilt up" and "tilt down," page 52

Cameramen as a whole do not get emotionally involved in the fine points of semantics. However, many find the use of "pan up" and "pan down" for "tilt up" and "tilt down" offensive. They hold that saying "pan" for vertical movement is a contradiction in terms.

24. Re: following action, page 53

A shot that follows action is also called a *follow shot.* This term used to be used for moving shots like the trucking shot discussed in Chapter 10, but when a pan follows *action,* it is just as much a follow shot.

25. Re: panning a static scene, page 53

Occasionally, there are dramatic reasons that justify panning a static scene. Examples: panning the members of a jury as they listen to testimony in a murder trial; or panning spectators at a football game from the point of view of a lost boy looking for his father.

26. Re: smooth pans, page 55
Smoothness applies both to the beginning and end of a pan. You may have to start or stop a pan suddenly—like shooting a baseball player stealing a base-but "suddenly" does not mean jerkily or unsteadily!

27. Re: panning from left to right and tilting from the bottom up, page 56
This caution applies mainly to static scenes and even here there can be exceptions, depending on what you want to emphasize or dramatize in the static scene. For instance, if you are going to shoot a legislator standing on the steps of the Capitol in order to make a statement to the press, you establish your scene dramatically by *tilting down* from the top of the dome to the man on the steps.

CHAPTER 9

28. Re: the trucking shot, page 59
You will hear this term used most often by older professional cameramen, especially when the camera is mounted on a dolly and moves on tracks. Indeed, British moviemakers still call it a *tracking* shot. However, there are cameramen who substitute the general term "moving shot" for the specific "trucking shot" (or "tracking shot"). This usage lacks precision but there's no great problem in living with it.

29. Re: rate of movement of the zoom lens, page 60
It is really the *image* that moves, not the zoom lens. Since it is part of the camera, the zoom lens remains stationary as long as the camera is stationary. So, strictly speaking, it is not a moving shot. However, we know the zoom lens produces a moving effect toward or away from the subject, so it is included in this chapter. As you've probably guessed, you can combine a moving shot with a zoom shot. This is not recommended, however, unless both shots start and stop at the same time. Otherwise there will be an abrupt change in the aparent motion in the frame as one shot ends and the other continues.

30. Re: the wide shot, page 61
Here is another source of fuzziness in terminology. The term "wide" shot is obviously derived from "wide-angle." it is heard constantly in television because of the enormous use of the wide-angle lens by TV studio cameramen. Unfortunately, one sometimes hears it used loosely in film. A director may order his cameraman to "cut to a wide shot" when he does not mean using a wide angle lens but moving the camera back from a relatively close shot to a longer shot. Example: cutting from a close shot of an individual in a group to a

full shot or long shot or the entire group. So, if you as a cameraman, hear your director call for a "wide shot," make sure you know exactly what he wants.

31. Re: abuse of the zoom lens, page 61
This is aptly derided as tromboning.

32. Re: using the zoom vs. walking the camera, page 61
Of course there are exceptions. When a TV news cameraman is shooting an interview, it would be most impractical for him to physically walk the camera in for a closer angle while the subject is speaking. In such a situation, and it is a very common one, the zoom lens is invaluable for its ease in obtaining a closeup—especially when the subject is saying something that warrants the visual emphasis of a CU.

Incidentally, it is the mark of an experienced cameraman that *before* zooming in, he shoots several seconds of the subject; and *after* zooming in, he shoots a similar amount from the close angle. It helps in editing.

33. Re: angle of view of the ordinary lens, page 62
This difference in angle of view of the ordinary lens is an advantage when you want the audience to be constantly aware of the environment through which the dolly shot is moving. Suppose the subject of the shot is the wealthy owner of a magnificent country estate who is standing at the far end of one of the gardens. The feeling of opulence is steadily enhanced as the camera moves in, its ordinary lens providing the eye with a rich, slowly passing panorama of beautiful flowers, hedges and statuary.

A zoom-in shot, though it can be made to move as slowly as a dolly-in, cannot be as effective. The rich breadth of view will inevitably be diminished as the zoom-in angle of view steadily narrows.

Also you lose the sense of changing perspective you get in a dolly shot, particularly if the foreground objects are relatively close to the camera. If you zoom by them, they simply go out of frame as the field of view narrows. In a dolly shot, the audience gets a sense of third dimension, of depth, as the foreground changes relative to the background.

This illustration justifies a cautionary word against impetuously abandoning long-used techniques because of the appearance of new equipment which seemingly outmodes them. And as it happens, the versatile zoom lens can be used for conventional dolly shots!

Think back to our first discussion of lenses in Chapter 7, The General Rule. We said that "the zoom lens combines the functions of the normal, the wide angle and the long lens." So you can set your zoom lens on a 16mm camera at 25mm and dolly in or out with it just as you would with an ordinary lens of fixed focal length.

CHAPTER 10

34. Re: distraction shots, page 67
Some cameramen prefer to call them "neutral" shots.

35. Re: screen direction, page 68
There is an appalling failure to mask changes in screen direction in many professional films, including Hollywood features and movies made for TV.

One wonders whether the moviemakers involved are careless, ignorant or lazy; or worst of all, that they feel their audiences won't notice the difference.

36. Re: the "two-shot," page 69
It is worth noting that the *two-shot*, or *three-shot* refers to specific persons (four people would more sensibly be called a *group shot)*); so they are always shot close or full to exclude anyone else from the shot. It would be misleading to call a long shot of Trudy and Dean playing tennis a two-shot; it would be correct if they were face-to-face at the net shaking hands.

37. Re: directional continuity, page 72
There is really no reason (unless dictated by plot or terrain) why the cowboys can't come from right to left and the Indians from left to right in the opening shots, as long as constant screen direction is maintained thereafter.

38. Re: clean exits, page 73
We are the first to admit that this practice is not always followed in feature films. Frequently several screen feet of a person exiting a scene are left in before the next scene appears. The contention being that it is enough to imply a complete physical exit; that showing a person still in the frame as he or she leaves ties the scenes together more strongly, creating a desirable tension between them. Since this reasoning is followed by seasoned professionals, we just can't climb on a pedantic high-horse and call it wrong. Nonetheless we can't help feeling that exits that aren't clean are like dangling threads that should be snipped off.

39. Re: blur pan, page 74
A blur pan quite a while back was also called a *swish pan.* Another synonym you may hear is *quick pan.* The blur pan no longer enjoys the popularity it once had among news cameramen. Maybe it was over-used. But it is a dynamic shot and the pendulum may swing back.

40. Re: the blur pan, page 74
You can easily make a blur pan by panning the car as it drives away, then

with the camera still running, go into an extremely fast pan in the direction the car is headed.

But you don't necessarily have to pan with a moving subject to get a good bour pan, although the sustained camera movement adds smoothness to the transition. Suppose you shoot a scene of a girl packing a bathing suit for a Florida vacation and you want a blur pan before the next shot showing her un-packing the bathing suit in a Florida setting. Well, a rapid pan of *any* kind of scene would give you an effective blur pan. You simply cut the packing shot in-to the beginning of the blur pan and the unpacking shot into the end of it.

By the way, you don't need much footage to get a blur pan. If you're shooting 16mm film a few feet—2 or 3 seconds—will do the trick; videotape is about the same.

41. Re: blur focus shot, page 75
You may, on occasion, hear it referred to as a *defocus* or *lose focus* shot. That's *lose,* not *"loose"!*

42. Re: blur focus again, page 75
Do *not* confuse blur focus with *soft focus.* Blur focus is a deliberate act by the cameraman to make the scene go out of focus completely. That is why you may hear a director tell his cameraman to "blur in" or "blur out."

In a *soft focus* shot, the image is still recognizable; but the focus isn't sharp. This is usually an unintentional error, due to lens or camera problems or the failure of the cameraman to check focus constantly.

There are occasions when the focus is deliberately softened slightly to create a romantic effect in lieu of other and better technical means of softening the image. Also deliberately, the focus may be softened a bit in so-called "sub-jective" camera shots in which the scene is shown through the eyes of a per-former, to suggest he or she is having trouble seeing clearly.

43. Re: optical effects, page 75
Do not confuse optical effects with special effects. Special effects refers to movie magic (miniatures, mattes, stop motion, etc.) that creates such dazzling visual images as King Kong perched on top of the Empire State Building or the futuristic space weaponry of *Star Wars.*

CHAPTER 11

44. Re: caution when shooting with video camera, page 90
Another caution when shooting video: avoid shooting a very light object against a dark background because if you pan, you will get an effect of light streaking or lag.

CHAPTER 12

45. Re: cut-ins, cut-aways and the film editor, page 94

No one appreciates the value of cut-ins and cut-aways for space/time jumps more than the editor.

Suppose he is cutting an important or dramatic event—the President's helicopter descending to the White House lawn, or a marathon runner pounding out the last mile to the finish. However, the action up to the climax—that is, the slow descent of the helicopter or the steady even plodding of the runner—can be tedious, dissipating the visual excitement of the event instead of sustaining it.

But, a cut-in of the whirling rotor blades, or a cut-away to spectators cheering the runner, will enable the film editor to cut to the descending helicopter just before it touches down, or to the runner only a few yards from the finish line, thus maintaining continuity, tempo and excitement.

Such cut-ins and cut-aways are pure gold to the TV news film editor who must cut a story to an extremely short running time—and do so very quickly.

46. Re: pictorial transitions and seeming jump cuts, page 95

You have to be careful when matching action in pictorial transitions to avoid what *seems to be* a jump cut because the subjects of the transition shots are look-alikes, as in the hand closeups.

In such a case it would be desirable to change the angle of the second shot, for example: shooting the CU of Johnny's hand in the ice cream parlor from a relatively high angle.

47. Re: matching action in overlap and pictorial transitions, page 95

This semantic confusion reveals a surprising gap in the usually precise language of pictorial continuity. The term "matching action" originated with overlap. Unfortunately, no new term has evolved to describe the special meaning of matching action in pictorial transitions. However, it should help to know that the term "overlap" automatically implies the kind of matching action used to avoid jump cuts.

48. Re: moviemaker's choice in pictorial transitions, page 95

To emphasize this point, we cheerfully contradict ourselves about the desirability of action transitions by saying that static shots can be just as effective. For instance, the shot right after the lawn-mowing sequence could be an extreme closeup of a dish of ice cream that is completely frame-filling. The camera pulls back—and we are in the ice cream parlor with the boys. Certainly this is a dramatic and pictorial transition, even if it lacks the action of the hands or bike wheel.

49. Re: combining pictorial and mechanical transitions, page 96

The closeups of the mother's wristwatch are actually pictorial transitions through matching action. Adding dissolves as mechanical transitions is not being redundant. Without the dissolve signaling transition in time, the audience might not have noticed that the wristwatch hands had moved.

Incidentally, a dissolve between two matching shots is called a *match dissolve.*

50. Re: straight cuts and tempo, page 97

Not so. Straight cuts do not significantly accelerate tempo. Tempo is a quality that emerges from how briskly a story seems to move within scenes and sequences. In other words, it is a function of action and dialogue. It is also, of course, determined by skill in editing.

51. Re: the straight cut, page 97

There are movie people who prefer the straight cut because they believe it is "modern" compared to "old-fashioned" pictorial or mechanical transitions. This is a naive belief. The straight cut was the practice in the early days of movie making, *before* pictorial and mechanical transitions were introduced. Which goes to prove there is nothing new under the sun, even in the relatively brief history of motion pictures.

The straight cut may have returned to contemporary movie making because of the television commercial which often deliberately abandons the rules of pictorial continuity. The idea is that jarring cuts create a powerful visual image that makes the sponsor's "message" a memorable one.

52. Re: bad straight cuts, page 97

Unfortunately, there are moviemakers who put no thought at all into making a straight cut, thinking that it's just a matter of splicing sequences together or just making good videotape edits. And if the transition is visually awkward and disrupts pictorial continuity, too bad—for the audience.

53. Re: the use of sound in straight-cut transitions, page 98

Some moviemakers who prefer straight cuts use sound (dialogue or sound effects) as a transitional device.

For example, a moviemaker may record a line of dialogue at the end of one sequence to introduce the next sequence. In the case of Freddy and Johnny, he might have Johnny say, when he receives the money from his mother, "Let's go get some ice cream"; then cut to them in the ice cream parlor.

Or he might use dialogue as a *sound bridge.* Freddy might answer Johnny by saying "That's a great idea, just great." The film records the first part of

Johnny's answer—"That's a great idea"—for the lawn scene; then cuts to the ice cream parlor where Freddy is heard finishing his answer with the exclamation "Just great!".

Sound used with a straight cut that works enhances the transition and will do the same for an appropriate pictorial or mechanical transition. In the case of a straight cut, the sound may divert attention from the gap in pictorial continuity. But don't deceive yourself. Sound used this way is a crutch, not a cure.

While we're on the subject of sound bridges, let's consider a special use of them which is, well, open to question. Let's call it overlapping sound—sound effects or dialogue that belongs to overlap the transition from the preceding sequence or the transition to the following sequence.

here's an example: The film shows Johnny and Freddy going from lawn to ice cream parlor with the turning bike wheel as a transition shot. Johnny's last line on the lawn is "let's go eat some ice cream." The film maker has the sound of the bike wheel fade in over Johnny's words, *before* the wheel. Conversely, he may have the wheel sound fade out *after* the boys are seen seated in the ice cream parlor talking about their treat.

This mismatch of sound to scene may be due to carelessness, but more often it is done deliberately by the film maker. He sincerely believes the overlapping sound makes the transition more dramatic and "tightens" continuity. Some audiences may accept this; others may feel irritated and slightly confused. Our answer? Well, think of what we said a while back about "clean entrances and exits."

CHAPTER 13

54. Re: manipulating tempo, page 105
To give credit where credit is due, some of the best examples of tempo manipulation are to be found in TV commercials, where the effect desired must be achieved in 10, 20, 30, or 60 seconds.

55. Re: slow or fast tempo, page 106
It is safe to say that an audience will be more quickly bored by a dragging tempo than it will be irritated by an over-fast tempo.

Film buffs may well ponder why, as films grew longer, good tempo seemed harder to achieve. Not many contemporary films, with their two-hour-plus length, have the drive and pace of the short silent films of the 1910s and 20s.

56. Re: film stories that keep moving, page 106
It is, strictly speaking, not a matter of tempo, but some movie stories that

keep moving never seem to stop—they are *too long!*

More than one well-done feature film has wearied its audience—and destroyed itself at the box office—by rambling on and on beyond the obvious ending. It is the moviemaker, not the story, that should be faulted. The reason is usually vanity—infatuation with the material he has shot—and a ruinous reluctance to cut it.

57. Re: parallax in video cameras, page 107

Not a problem in today's video cameras since their viewfinders are of the through-the-lens (T-T-L) type.

58. Re: composition, page 109

When shooting for television, it is important to know that the TV set cuts off as much as 13 percent of the border *all around the frame.* This fact is not particularly worrisome in long shots, but it certainly is in tight shots.

Unawareness of this fact may account for some cameramen unwittingly slicing off parts of their subjects when shooting CUs or ECUs.

59. Re: cameramen and film editor, page 111

The TV news cameraman who fails to provide adequate coverage for the editor imposes a severe hardship on the man in the editing room, who must often work against the clock to prepare a story by air time. The lack of inserts and buildup shots makes it very difficult for even the most resourceful film editor to put together the story with good continuity—especially when the cameraman's coverage runs long but the edited story must be very brief!

(*See* footnote 45 on "cut-ins, cut-aways and the film editor" in Trims and Out-Takes.)

60. Re: tape recorded in the field, page 112

Unsurprisingly, this is also termed the *field tape.*

61. Re: "master" and "slave," page 112

Since the tape on which the final edits are laid down is called the "master," some video engineers like to call the tape that is played back for re-recording the "slave tape."

62. Re: re-recording and "dubbing" videotape, page 112

Making a copy of an edited video master tape is called "dubbing" and the product is a "dub," just as an answer print in film is made from an edited master negative.

We stress this specific meaning in video because dubbing is an old familiar term in the world of audio in connection with sound tracks.

CHAPTER 14

63. Re: leftover unexposed film, page 118

A short length of unexposed film at the end of an exposed reel, too brief for shooting a complex take of a scene, is known unsurprisingly as a *short end*. It may be used for tests; to shoot additional inserts; or simply "run out," that is, shot as superfluous footage at the tail end of the last acene.

64. Re: being a moviemaker as well as a cameraman, page 124

This text was written primarily for the beginner at moviemaking, the man or woman who wants to know how to use a film or video camera to shoot a movie story. But we hope we have made it clear that to make a good movie, the beginner must be more than a cameraman; he must become, even in an elementary sense, a moviemaker.

This means that he must perform other functions besides operating the camera. He must think in terms of story, so he is serving himself as a scenario writer, even though his "writing" may be nothing more than mental advance planning. We stressed that he should also think—and perform—as an editor, constantly bearing in mind how his edited footage will appear onscreen. Since in most instances, he controls the action he is shooting, he becomes a director, even though a rudimentary one. And when he picks a particular setting whether outdoors or indoors, rearranges the furniture in a room or asks his performers to change an article of clothing, he is emulating the actions of an art director and scenic designer even though he may not realize it.

Combining all these functions in the single person of the beginner is possible because he is making movies in a ver limited way, at his leisure and convenience, free of the pressures of time and money, for the amusement of himself, his family and friends. Even the serious young moviemaker who has professional aspirations can, if he chooses his subject carefully, be a movie jack of all trades.

However if the beginner eventually becomes a professional, he finds that he can no longer function as a one-man team. The degree of expertise required in each of the many aspects of commercial moviemaking is too high, its mechanics and economics so complex and costly that there must be a division of labor. So he finds a variety of professional specialists practicing the different skills he combined lightly in his head as a beginner. The best of these are more than highly skilled technicians, they are also creative artists, whose functions are indispensable to movie making.

It is important that he remembers this if his goal is to become the most glamorous and prestigious of all the specialists behind the camera—the director. There is no question about the overall authority of the director. He is the decision maker in the countless details of production, the coordinator of the many moviemaking activities that go on simultaneously, the controller of the specialists behind the camera as well as the performers in front of it.

He also has a vital creative role since he is the catalyst for the various talents collaborating on the movie; he is their enhancer and, frequently, a direct collaborator; the final product may bear the imprint of his own unique style.

There is a cult of movie buffs who go far beyond this. They romanticize the director as the sole creative force disregarding the other creative contributors as not only subordinate but minor. The young moviemaker must fight to resist this flattery.

The point is not that it is unfair, but that it is wholly unrealistic. The director is (or should be!) the creative leader of the moviemaking team; without that team he cannot function as a director. The would-be director who ignores this basic fact of life does so at his peril.

65. Re: fashions in moviemaking, page 124

Another recurring fashion is deliberate ambiguity. Cloudiness of plot or meaning may titillate audience curiosity at first, but it is dangerous if the ambiguity is not ultimately resolved—if the moviemaker puts the burden of making sense out of his film on the audience.

The average audience will resent the idea of doing the movie maker's work for him (even if the ambiguity is not deliberate!). It may retaliate by losing interest. There's no punishment worse than that to a moviemaker.

66. Re: the importance of sound, page 126

We don't want to end this book with the impression that although sound is subordinate to picture in a movie story, that it plays a *minor* role. Not so at all. Good dialogue, good sound effects, good music, can play powerful—even key—roles. They add realism and believability, heighten dramatic and emotional effect, increase visual impact.

We are not disparaging the importance of sound when we criticize its use to camouflage poor pictorial technique. It doesn't work, anyway. Skillfully used sound makes the faults of a poorly made movie stand out in contrast. How often have you left a theatre with little of the picture in your mind, but recalling with pleasure clever dialogue, striking sound effects, a catchy title song or a rich musical score? Enough said.

BREAKING INTO THE FIELD: SOME TIPS

BY WAY OF INTRODUCTION

As interest in film and video mushroomed in recent years, it was inevitable that many young people would seek employment in these visual media. So we were not surprised to receive inquiries on how to go about hunting for a job.

Our response to date was a polite negative. The theme of this book is pictorial continuity, not employment counseling. Nor did we want any reader to mislead himself into thinking that whatever advice we could give would in any way guarantee employment.

Nor were we encouraged to change our minds by the fact that many inquirers made it clear, whether they realized it or not, that their real interest was not in the craft or creative process of film or video but in finding a job that would pay well, plus the bonus of working in a so-called "glamorous field."

Don't get us wrong, there's nothing wrong with these motives, nothing at all! But after many years in film and television, we feel there is something very special to vocations in these fields and that those who pursue them should be animated by more than just the desire for a good pay check, which can be found in other fields as well. So we hope you understand why the purely glamour- (and money-hunting) job seeker just didn't "turn us on."

However, we have come to believe that those job seekers interested in earning "big bucks" are now outnumbered by young men and women who have a genuine deep interest in and affection for film and video, that they have a drive to be achievers in a very demanding but fulfilling profession, that they want to be—and be known as—craftsmen and artists, as true professionals whose love for their work means as much as the money or status it brings.

So we have written the following chapter for these dedicated young hopefuls. Perhaps it will make it a little easier to track that elusive quarry—a "working assignment." For that is all these job tips can do—point you in the right direction and, perhaps, save you some time, effort and disappointment.

The odds against you are devastating. You'll be competing against thousands of men and women who took film and videotape courses in hundreds of schools and colleges throughout the country and who have the same goal in mind. In the case of TV news, it gets harder and harder for an outsider to break into the heavily staffed news departments of big-city stations.

So if you do succeed in your job hunt, it will be *your* energy and determination, *your* imagination and craftsmanship, that did the trick!

THE FIRST COMMANDMENT

Before you begin looking for a job, be sure you *know your stuff.* If you've read this book, you are by now saturated with the admonition to learn pictorial continuity. And if you've picked up our book for the first time and turned immediately to this supplement be assured there is no point in your reading it unless you familiarize yourself with the technique that is the lifeblood of film and video making.

We have another admonition that is no less important: know your equipment and materials—your cameras, lenses, batteries and other accessories, your film and videotape raw stock. Know how they work and why, what they can do for you and what they can't.

Even a little academic knowledge, let's say just the rudiments, of the laws of chemistry, optics and electronics that govern shooting film and tape, is not a bad idea. No, such knowledge isn't necessary to get good footage, but it will help by increasing your self-confidence when you use your complex working tools.

Okay? Now let's get on track.

IT'S A COLD, CRUEL WORLD

If you have friends or relatives in film or television influential enough to get you a job as a cameraman (or as a director or producer), congratulations! You don't have to read any further.

Likewise, if you have the connections or salesmanship and patience (lots of patience!) to persuade one of the numerous government and private foundations, endowments, cultural or arts councils to provide you with a money grant to shoot a film or videotape story, well, great! You, too, have it made.

However, if you do not have such an advantage; if you are nonetheless eager to become a professional cameraman; if you are ready to go through fire, fatigue, frustration and ferocious disappointment to achieve your dream and so spend many, many months, even years, striving for it—why, then, read on and more power to you!

Make no mistake. This is one of the most difficult professions to crack. It is important that you develop a tough mental and emotional attitude so that you can shake off the job disappointments, near-misses, snubs, slights and cold, unfeeling rejections that will inevitably come your way.

If you are easily hurt or depressed by failure; or quick to anger or to get impatient because of frustration; then you are in for a rough time, very rough.

Nor will psychological pressures and stresses lessen once you are established professionally; they will simply assume a different form. You will have to stand up to tensions caused by unexpected delays and seemingly endless waiting, by the gremlins and bugs that inhabit film and video equipment and seem to reproduce their kind. No, this profession is not for high-strung people who are vulnerable to stress-caused afflictions like ulcers, hemorrhoids and the like.

Which leads to another caveat: stay in good physical shape. Your job may put you on an assignment that runs far beyond normal working hours. You can count on being on your feet for hours at a time, while carrying *and* operating equipment that adds up to substantial bulk and weight, even though the trend is toward smaller, lighter equipment.

Also, forget about regular meals, especially eating lunch at a set time. Forget, too, about going to the men's or ladies' room just because you feel the need. You will be able to go only when your work allows you to.

If you have chronic problems involving heart, stomach or bladder, think twice before seeking a cameraman's career. And if we seem rather blunt in describing this problem, we apologize; but we feel that you should know the facts of life.

All in all, you have a better chance of living a long, productive life as a moviemaker if you have an iron constitution, an unending supply of patience, energy, good humor and at least a little of that wonderful knack of letting trials and tribulations run off you like water off a duck's back.

Are you discouraged by all these warnings? Of course not! Now that we've told you the worst, and you haven't blinked an eye, we must admit that these problems do not affect all types of camera work to the same degree.

The most vulnerable are TV news cameramen. Not only do they work against the TV clock, but when their stories are of a "one time only" nature, they must get their shots on the first try, with no chance of a second take.

Obviously, the pressures will be far less on cameramen or camerawomen who have ample shooting schedules on stories for business firms, government agencies, industrial or educational institutions or non-profit organizations such as foundations, museums, professional societies and so on.

We figure that most of our readers who hope to make their livelihood as camerapersons are aiming for TV, at least initially. So they are the target of our opening remarks. Please don't feel we've snubbed you if TV is not your goal. What we have to say in this chapter applies in some degree to *all* categories of camera work.

MUST YOU HAVE A VIDEO CAMERA?

Most TV news is now shot on videotape. Its use in documentaries is increasing; likewise in business and other types of films not made specifically for television.

You might think that it would be an advantage, as an aspiring cameraman, if you owned your own video rig. Unfortunately, the prices are fantastic. A complete rig, with camera, recorder and accessories, sells in the lower-to-mid five-figure range and may very well go up with inflation. You know what the cost of bank loans is these days, so unless you have a rich and indulgent parent or other relative, buying new equipment may be only a dream.

Used equipment is cheaper; its cost can be half as low as the price of the brand new item, but there is a big "but." The minicam is a highly sophisticated electronic instrument. If you do not have the maintenance know-how, you could inherit more problems than the savings are worth.

There is another factor to consider—obsolescence. The videotape camera and its related equipment is in a state of steady, rapid change. It is evolving toward smaller size and less weight; toward greater efficiency and reliability of operation. That's fine, of course, but what you buy this year may be obsolete next year, literally, and you know what that would do to the resale value of your rig.

Film equipment, on the other hand, has been in development many years—a good half-century longer. It has evolved to a state where it remains relatively constant and standardized, especially the camera itself.

So have no fear about being stuck with an "old-fashioned" film camera. TV stations will retain film facilities for a long time to come; ditto with non-broadcast audio/visual organizations. *They have to.*

Film and tape will co-exist, comfortably, far into the future. One of the happy features of this coexistence is that if the visual material is shot on film but distribution requirements call for video the film can be transferred to tape with the greatest of ease. Unfortunately the converse is not true, for now. At this time, transferring tape to film is more difficult, more expensive, and the quality often unsatisfactory.

The advent of videotape did shake up the communications world. It is a wonderful visual medium unbeatable for speed and the feeling of "immediacy" it conveys. Some people held it to be inevitable that tape would mainly supplant film for television use.

Except for hard news that just hasn't happened. Producers of made-for-TV movies, big-budget commercials and even documentaries have switched back to film. Some reasons for this switchback concern cost and reliability of operation in the field. A major concern, however is "the film look." This is a certain quality, an appeal, that is unique to film just as immediacy is unique to tape.

¾" videotape camera
(Ikegami)

Many producers like the happy compromise of shooting on film and editing the product on tape.

Let's get down to some bedrock truisms: both the film and video camera are in the business of producing a succession of visual images. The requirements for skilled operation are the same (framing, panning, following action, etc.), the need for understanding the fundamentals of lighting is the same; and above all, the technique of pictorial continuity is the same.

You will find cameramen who, for personal reasons, prefer one camera over the other. You may make such a choice yourself. Fine. Just don't deceive yourself into thinking that either one will do a better job for you in terms of pictorial continuity. No way! That technique is in your head, not in the equipment. It is the cameraman who takes the pictures, not the camera!

A GEOGRAPHICAL NOTE

We hope that you do not intend to hunt for a job in a giant metropolitan area like New York City, Boston, Washington D.C., Dallas, Detroit, Chicago, or Los Angeles. Apart from the obstacles we've already mentioned, you may run into union problems and other complications that can make job-hunting a nightmare.

16mm film camera
(Arriflex)

You have a better chance of selling yourself and your skills if you are located in or near a medium-size city with TV stations affiliated with the major commercial networks. A public broadcasting station within the same general area gives you another market for your wares.

The same holds true for the non-broadcast field. Hundreds upon hundreds of small business firms specializing in film and tape audio visual (A/V, for short) production for business and industry have sprung up in every corner of the country. Check the Yellow Pages of your local phone book for names. Their number may surprise you.

Many industrial giants, and quite a few medium-size business enterprises, have their own in-house A/V departments that produce films and video tapes for sales, personnel training, advertising and public information. Check them out. If their answer is "We don't have in-house facilities," ask who does their contract work in film or tape.

While you're at it, make the same inquiries of advertising agencies and public relations firms. They are also involved in film and tape media.

Tell yourself that you are going to run down any and all leads. Sure the average one is a long shot, especially when you try it cold, without benefit of a contact or introduction. But luck and timing do play a part sometimes. The only way of increasing the odds in your favor is to keep plugging away. You really have no choice, if you want to break into movie making.

YOUR FOOT IN THE DOOR

We trust you realize that ambition, persistence, good intentions and some knowledge gained through college or tech school communications courses will not, in themselves, gain you entree anywhere. The best you can hope for is a more or less polite answer of "Come back when you have experience."

Experience! That is your greatest asset in the job hunt. It is a must. Without it, the trail you pursue will go in circles or peter out entirely.

Take note that by "experience," we mean commercial experience. We do not belittle the "hands on" experience you can gain working with commercial-type equipment at school. That is valuable in familiarizing you with equipment and technique, including—we hope—pictorial continuity.

True, there is a handful, a *handful*, of prestigious film schools—chiefly on the West Coast—whose graduation certificate commands respect. These schools, however, are oriented toward feature film production. Moreover, the competition to get in is formidable.

You have a right to say that the problem is similar to the question of "Which came first—the chicken or the egg?" You need experience to get a job but you can't get a job without experience!

There are solutions. One solution works for a surprising number of people. It may also work for you if . . . The "if" is *if* you have patience, *if* you do not insist on a film- or video-related job right away (let alone starting off as a cameraman or assistant cameraman!), *if* you are willing to first "pay your dues" with a job or jobs that may be dull, poorly paid and which may involve long hours and hard work.

They are sometimes called "entry level jobs," a euphemism for starting at the foot of the ladder. But they do get your foot "inside the door"; they can open the way to doing camera work in time, *if* you give them a chance.

All organizations involved in film or television production to any degree (we mentioned them under "A Geographical Note") have a constant need for people who are ready to assume the chores, the menial housekeeping tasks, the "donkey work" that keeps an organization going. The job may be filing film or tape clips, being a messenger, clerking in an office or supply room or working in a warehouse.

Obviously the rewards are small in pay or satisfaction, but you are *on the inside*; with persistence, tact and a little luck, you can work your way around to the production or camera departments.

Consider that word "luck." It is not a throwaway reference. Luck plays a part in this profession as it does in any other. We believe that you give your luck a boost by working doggedly at your goal and by believing in yourself and your future. This is not a profession in which good luck happens to people who look down on themselves as chronic losers.

Luck is at work if you happen to attend a college which has an intern program with a local TV station and you qualify for it. What's lucky is that being an intern gets you past the security guard at the front door. Don't let the title "intern" create great expectation. The job may be only remotely connected (if at all) with shooting or other production work. Interning may demand a lot of your time with little—or no—pay and certainly no guarantee of employment at the end.

However, you are *inside*. You can move around, make contacts. And there is a form of interning that offers real opportunity, that of being appointed a newsroom desk assistant. Sure, that's a dressed up version of the older, plainer term of copy boy, errand boy or "gofer." But you are at the heart of the news action, you can learn a lot, and you can make contact with cameramen, editors and other specialists in TV news production. Interning can be a modest entry in your record of experience.

Okay, suppose you think this "back door" approach isn't for you for any of a variety of reasons. Suppose you've been unable to find an entry level job; or suppose you have an entry level job, believe you've given it a fair shot but are dissatisfied with your chances of doing camera work; or perhaps your entry level job has given you a small amount of genuine experience but you want to speed up your progress; or you may feel you'd rather gamble on convincing a prospective employer or your potential ability so that he will hire you for a camera-related job even without working experience. Quite a gamble—you'd have to be powerfully persuasive—but you may feel justified in taking it.

What to do?

THE SAMPLE REEL OR CASSETTE

You do what job seekers in many other fields do—provide samples of your wares. For instance, artists looking for jobs as illustrators have portfolios with various examples of their work. In your case, it would be three or four stories dubbed "a sample reel" whether it's film on a reel or videotape in a cassette.

Your sample reel should be tailored as much as possible to the needs of a prospective employer. Most audiovisual production houses will take on any kind of assignment. Quite a few, though, tend to specialize in line with the specific products of their biggest and most profitable clients. These may range widely through the industrial world (chemicals, automotive, data-processing, etc.) and the non-industrial (travel, teaching, wild life, etc.)

So it's a good idea to check out the track record of the A/V company you've targeted for a job before putting together your sample reel.

If, despite our grim warnings, your prime goal remains TV news, it stands to reason that one of your most important samples would be a suddenly breaking story—a fire or accident, a street demonstration or riot. This will show your ability to react to the unexpected, to record that "instant only," never-to-be-repeated shot that may well be the heart of the story. At the same time, it should show your ability to get the cut-ins and cut-aways necessary for building *and* for editing the story.

Another desirable sample is that of a news story that is timely or topical but has been organized in advance, like a July 4th parade or the demonstration of a new automobile safety device. Pre-arranged news events like these enable you to plan your shooting for greatest effectiveness and economy.

Then, of course, there is the feature story. Features range from novelties—a new fashion, a new toy—to stories with strong human interest. They contain elements that will involve viewers and even cause them to identify with the subject. The choice is practically limitless: a person of very advanced age—perhaps 90 or more—celebrating a birthday, triplets or quadruplets just born to their stunned parents, a pretty young lady who's won a beauty contest, a local athlete training for a big meet, a wife/mother who's written a cookbook, a policeman or fireman hero, and so on.

The unusual always holds interest—an 85-year-old mountain climber, for instance (we've met one). The same 85-year-old gyrating in front of a rock band would be even more unusual. It could also be grotesque and in bad taste.

Chances are you will run across possible feature stories or other news items that are on the borderline—or beyond—of good taste; or which may go against community ethical, moral or religious standards, or at least you think that they might. So you are in a dilemma.

Now, ever since photojournalism was born, print media have used material that is sensational, shocking or in dubious taste as long as it was deemed newsworthy. TV news, which depicts these qualities even more vividly, has followed suit since its inception. There are limits, of course. Stories of an explicit sexual nature, which lean heavily on the sado-masochistic or which seem to wallow in gore or violence will probably be ruled out by the station or network's own code of "standards and practices."

A cameraman assigned to cover a sensational story does not worry about matters of taste. He shoots the story and lets his superiors make the judgment of whether it goes on the air or not.

There is the answer to your dilemma. If you have a strong story for your sample reel but have doubts about its sensational aspects, shoot it and let your prospective employer pass judgment on it. He may decide against using it, but if he likes it he'll remember you the next time around. Of course if he suspects that you have gone out of your way to over-emphasize the sensational—possibly distorting the story for that purpose—he'll remember you too, but not the way you want to be.

Let's get back on the track of human interest stories. As we said, the unusual always holds interest. But don't pass by the ordinary or commonplace as dull or uninteresting subjects. Subjects involving health, leisure, inflation, self-fulfillment, family matters—anything to do with how people live and work—are always of potential interest.

The trick is to give a fresh look to the familiar, to touch the emotions of viewers or give them an interesting insight or piece of information. A TV news feature about a cleaning woman was a prize-winning network story!

Some features have a degree of timeliness and must be on the air within a limited time period or become stale—like the beauty contest winner—but this doesn't matter when you're using the story as part of a sample reel.

Nor does a feature have to be about a person or animal. It could be about an unusual object—a historic landmark, an antique automobile, a rare flower.

But beware. These objects are static, inanimate. It takes an advanced order of skill and creativeness to make them come alive. Graphic buildup shots, careful lighting, a discreet, balanced use of panning and moving shots, all these can be of great help in getting rid of that "static cling"!

Only don't get carried away. Make your story look as good as it can; but don't get so finicky with fine photography that your feature appears to have been shot in a studio. It would then look out of key with your other news stories; it would look too calculated instead of fresh and spontaneous.

It helps to have a person in the story even if he or she is just an observer or visitor. It lightens the static nature of your subject; it gives the camera a legitimate reason to follow the person around, or to go into a closeup to show in detail what the visitor is looking at. Take care about using a pretty girl—she may distract the viewer from your subject! At least cut away from her frequently, so your viewer sees what you want him to see.

Don't feel unequal to the challenge if you decide against shooting a feature story on a static subject. They *are* difficult to bring off. Nor is the return worth it if it appears that it will take an excessive amount of time and effort as well as skill. You may be better off choosing another type of feature for your sample reel.

Incidentally, never think of a news feature as a "mini-documentary." That's a misleading, harmful term. It suggests the wrong kind of approach, one that is expository or interpretive. That's appropriate for a documentary, but not a news story which is strictly reportage.

QUALITY CONTROL

We take it for granted that the stories in your sample reel will be technically first-rate, carefully shot and edited, and put together with observance of the principles of pictorial continuity. Here are some guidelines to keep your quality high. They apply to any sample reel, regardless of the film or videotape field you're interested in.

Omit flawed shots. You may have a great action sequence, but if the focus is fuzzy or the continuity jumpy, including such material suggests that you do not know any better; or even worse, that your prospective employer doesn't!

Keep your sample stories short. Visual verbosity is as much a fault in screen photography as wordiness is in written material. Whoever is going to look at your sample reel already has a full work load without viewing your stuff; and there may be sample reels from other applicants for him or her to screen!

If you are trying to crack TV news in particular, brevity is more than a necessity; it is the strongest kind of imperative. Time the stories on your favorite TV news programs. Most run one minute plus some seconds; few are two minutes or more; major news events and sports are the few exceptions.

It's not a bad idea to shoot a series of learning exercises till you get the knack of covering a story with a minimum of film or tape. You'll also learn an invaluable lesson of how much information you can get—smoothly—into a small time frame.

Edit the stuff yourself. You'll see how indispensable cut-ins and cut-aways are for eliminating unnecessary footage. Nothing irritates a film or video tape editor more than to receive 30 minutes of footage for a one minute story, then have to hunt frantically for cut-aways to trim the story to time and still have it hang together.

Stay out of the film. Let the story be the story, not you! Don't make your sample reel a vehicle for an ego trip. This admonition is directed specifically at would-be cameramen and moviemakers.

We were tempted to say that if you want a job *on* camera you are reading the wrong book; but we'd have to eat our words if the reader turned out to be someone whose goal was to be a news correspondent. (There are cameramen/reporters, too). In that case you would do yourself a service by acquainting yourself with the principles of pictorial continuity.

Most big-city stations do not send out a field producer or director with news camera crews on a local story. As a news correspondent, you may be out in the field supervising the shooting of your story, then wind up in the editing room overseeing its cutting. So knowing what continuity is all about will help your story to look good.

TO WHOM IT MAY CONCERN

Okay, you've put together what you consider is a good sample reel. Question: just to whom do you send it?

To begin with, try to personalize your submission. That is, don't just address your work sample to the president or audiovisual (A/V) production chief. Get their names and precise titles and get the spelling right! It's easy to find out this information. Often a polite call to the company switchboard will do it; you can also look up the information in trade publications or in client directories put out by audiovisual magazines. Try to check out the person directly responsible for A/V media. Usually a company president is far more involved with product, sales, and policy than with A/V matters.

Of course if the company business is A/V production, it's fairly simple to target your man or woman. Usually these production houses have small staffs, with just a few officers.

If the company is a big-product manufacturer or service organization, do a little more digging. If it has an in-house A/V unit, send your work sample to the unit head. However, the company may contract with an advertising agency for all its visual media needs. The agency, in turn, may contract with an A/V production house. So you skip the company's advertising director and the ad agency; then zero in on the production house. That's where the work is.

Be sure to send a polite but business-like cover note with the reel. A resume? Okay, if it shows some solid credits; it may hurt, though, if it's so skimpy it marks you painfully as a beginner. And make sure you include a caption sheet in which you *tersely* describe what each item is about. You don't want to irritate a prospective employer by making him wonder about the nature of some of your shots.

It's a good idea to include return postage. If you want it returned insured or registered, include the appropriate amount. Otherwise, it may be sent back at the lowest and slowest rate, or not at all. Which brings us to a vital caveat: *Never send out your only copy of your sample reel.* Get yourself a duplicate print or a tape dub of your work.

Now what if you're trying to crack a television station? Well, hiring power is almost always the prerogative of the news director. On a big, busy station he may delegate that power to an assistant news director.

These top people usually rely heavily on the judgment of the person who would be the hiree's immediate supervisor. In hiring a news writer or correspondent, that person would be the executive producer, producer or a senior news editor; for film or tape editors it would be their supervisory editor; for camera crews it would be the camera crew supervisor or someone who functions in that capacity. Smaller stations may not have a camera crew supervisor; the assignment editor may double in that function, or for that matter, the assistant news director. His chief responsibility may be personnel of all kinds.

You can resolve the question of who the camera crew supervisor or his surrogate is by calling up the newsroom and asking. If the answer is ambiguous or otherwise unsatisfactory, send your sample reel to the news director. His secretary will see that it gets into the right hands. The same considerations about a cover note, postage, etc., apply.

If you'd like to check out the lay of the land more carefully before submitting your sample reel, you might think of making contact with the station's news cameramen to find out what's going on inside their shop. Don't expect help from a free-lancer; he'll probably consider you as a potential competitor!

If you do get hold of a cooperative cameraman, he may even let you go out with him on a story he's covering—an excellent learning experience. But this is a dubious gambit in cities where cameramen are unionized. Your contact may be sympathetic (he was a beginner once, too) but union work-rules forbid a non-union person accompanying a union crew in a learner capacity. It's conceivable that the union might have an apprentice system, but you'd have to look into that.

Incidentally, if you hope to shoot for a television station that is unionized, bear in mind that you will have to join the union whether you work as a staff member or free-lancer.

You may ask: Why not deliver the sample reel in person once you get a firm fix on who should get it? Fine idea—nothing like eye contact with a prospective employer—but chancy. You're not going to get past the security people guarding the entrance unless you have an appointment. However, the receptionist may call your potential employer to find out whether he'll see you anyway. If the answer is no, the receptionist will see that your sample reel is picked up and delivered to him. If you try this "in person" approach, do it early in the day. News people get awfully busy as air time approaches.

If you're gambling on an interview, dress neatly. You don't have to wear a three-piece vested suit, just look your best. A lot of camera crew persons (as well as newsroom people) like to indulge themselves in wild or sloppy dress. Nobody seems to mind that, but wait till you're employed before taking off sartorially.

Once you believe your sample reel is in the right hands, allow a reasonable time for a reaction. If you press for an answer prematurely, or—much worse—pester your target with notes or phone calls, you are likely to blow your chances.

If several weeks have passed and you've heard nothing, a polite inquiry is in order. If you still hear nothing, ask for your reel back. This may push your target into screening your reel, or for asking for more time in which to screen it, or you may get it back without any communication whatsoever.

If the last situation occurs, don't lose your cool. You may feel you've been unfairly dealt with—and you may have genuine reason to think so—but swallow the slight (which most likely was never meant intentionally); accept it as one of those things a beginner must contend with.

Don't pop off with an angry letter or telephone call! You won't get much relief from it—the rebuff will still chafe—and you may get yourself marked as a sorehead. The wheel of fortune does turn, you may get another chance at the same place later on and it's no help to have someone inside who remembers you unfavorably.

As Shakespeare—or was it Confucius?—once said, somewhat confusingly: "Better to have a friend than an enemy; and if not a friend, then better not an enemy."

P.S. If you put what you've just read about the sample reel together with what you read earlier about entry level jobs, it adds up to a simple fact: that it's much easier to place that sample reel in the right hands when you're working *inside* the organization.

KEEP SHOOTING

All right, your reel has reached the TV news camera crew supervisor, he likes your work, you've received word that he's recommended you to the assignment editor.

Don't expect a staff job to follow! Be pleased that you'll get a crack at freelance assignments or perhaps you'll be asked to work as a stringer. Definition: A stringer is still a free-lancer but he's on call to cover a certain area just like reporters. The area may be the suburb of a big city; or it may be a small town (possibly where you live) which does not have its own TV station but which is covered by the nearest station whose broadcasts reach the town.

So what do you do now that you're on the assignment editor's list? Sit around and watch TV until "the man" calls you? Of course not! You keep on shooting!

What you do is go out and get the kind of story the station would want to run but which, for whatever reason, it did not get or could not get.

True, that's more easily said than done, but there are ways. One way is to have short-wave radio equipment, preferably mobile, that will enable you to listen in on the frequencies used for police emergency calls. These will also mention fire alarms. The same equipment should help you tune in on the short-wave bands used by all types of radio news dispatchers to communicate with their people in the field. (If you manage to get friendly with a news cameraman, he may even tell you the precise frequency his outfit uses.)

By the way, avoid the beginner label by never using the terms "radio" or "short-wave" in referring to this equipment. They are always known as "scanners" and scan from 8 to 16 channels.

If you haven't got the scanner or can't afford to buy it even though the item is relatively cheap now, think of cultivating a police contact at your precinct station or at headquarters. This should be someone, uniformed or a civilian, who will know when something big is about to break and can get word to you right away. That can be a very valuable contact and if you establish it, keep it flourishing by showing your appreciation.

As for non-urgent news events, the pre-planned ones, there's nothing like the first edition of your daily newspaper or an early morning broadcast on your radio station (could be your local TV station, too) to find out what's going on in town.

Okay, let's say that things break your way and you learn that TV news cameramen are going to cover a particular fire or accident. Does this mean you rush out and shoot the same story? No! Don't try to compete with the station's cameramen. They will not appreciate it, their assignment editors will not appreciate it, their news producers will not appreciate it. Don't commit the fatal error of trying to prove you're better than any cameraman they've got (at least, not before you're well-established!).

The whole point is to shoot a usable story that the station's cameramen will *not* be covering. If you know that they're at a particular fire or accident, stay away. In any sizable city or built-up area, you can count on more than one daily fire, accident or other emergency that qualifies as hard news.

Even a big station's camera crews are limited in number. So is its list of approved free-lancers. If they're all tied up on other stories, it's an opportunity for you to submit an "exclusive."

However, please run a possible exclusive through your news sense—and common sense—for an appraisal of its true story value before you commit time, energy and film or tape to it.

This is what we mean: a police car will respond to a fender-bender auto collision, but there's no story for you in the drivers exchanging licenses and insurance certificates. On the other hand, if a car is overturned and ties up traffic during the rush hour, *that's* a story.

Another example: firemen putting out a rubbish blaze doesn't add up to much that's newsworthy. It will add up to a lot of story, however, if there are flammable chemicals in the rubbish that may catch fire and spread flames to nearby buildings.

Here's a different angle for you to consider. A spectacular event like a big fire is a major news story the day it happens but the next day it is old news. Yet there may be a follow-up event that would give it a fresh angle. Suppose the fire burnt out many buildings. Going back the next day to shoot the rubble and debris (some of it still smoldering), with former tenants poking about searching for their possessions, would make a strong sequel.

Or perhaps what's left standing of the buildings is in danger of collapse and may be pulled down. Building demolition always makes a spectacular footage. It has the potential for an exciting follow-up story.

How do you find out if and when such a demolition will take place? You check the public officials who would be involved. Such agencies as police, fire or housing are obvious. Give it a bit of thought, though, and you will realize that sewage mains, water and power lines may also be affected and the municipal departments concerned with them would also be in the know about demolition plans. Train yourself to think broadly and imaginatively about sources of information.

In general, it's a good idea to get to know local government officials as widely as possible. In a highly organized society as ours, any activity affecting the public welfare would come under the supervision or control of public officials. They are aware of events past, present and pending—the long-term, career people can be mines of information—and they are usually happy to be of help especially if the effort will help the taxpayer's awareness (and appreciation) of their services.

The same holds true for private organizations—cultivate them! Let them know you're always interested in tips that may lead to shooting a news story. Start building yourself a network of "tipsters," like most old pros have.

It may have occurred to you that it's much easier to build such a network in a modestly sized city rather than a giant one like Denver or Cleveland, let alone a megalopolis (we checked the spelling) like New York or Chicago.

Got it all so far? Good! Let's go back to class again . . .for a moment.

FUNDAMENTALS! FUNDAMENTALS!

So now, by expending energy, imagination, ingenuity as well as time, gasoline, telephone calls, etc., you are about to shoot a story, one that will get your foot inside that door marked "Professionals Only."

Before you begin, take a deep breath and loosen up. Don't let anxiety or pressure make you forget everything you've learned. Shoot with deliberation even when you have to shoot fast. Think ahead! Organize your story so that it has a beginning, a middle and an end!

Shoot enough cut-aways!

Avoid needless zooms and pans!

Keep your camera steady!

Shoot enough closeups!

Do these admonitions sound familiar? Of course! They are among the fundamentals of pictorial continuity. Yet it's surprising that many professional cameramen forget them at times.

Don't let lapses by professionals lead you to think that you as a beginner can get away with the same thing. The cliché that you're only as good as your last job is too true even if that job is your hundredth, regardless of whether it's a news story, a documentary, an industrial film or a feature film. Do a sloppy job just once and that's what will be remembered, not the good work you did before. Yes, Shakespeare said something about that, too.

One more must: when you turn in a film or video story, make sure the vital statistics go along with it in the form of a caption or notes. These should have complete and accurate names and addresses, plus briefly, the who, what, when, where, why and how that are the basics of any kind of reporting.

ABOUT SHOOTING DOCUMENTARIES

We're sure that at this point there are readers who will say all this is well and good, but we want to shoot (and/or produce or direct) documentaries, not news. Which way do we go?

The answer, regretfully, is that there is no direct trail. It's even tougher to beat your way to a documentary job than it is to news. That's not because documentaries are a higher order of camera work, or pay more, or are more prestigious. It's that there are fewer markets, fewer opportunities, fewer jobs. It is *not* the way to go for those who hope to make a living early on in their careers.

The cameramen whose names appear on network documentary credits have established themselves over a long period of time. Some of them have been at it since the '50s and '60s. *And* most of them won their spurs as news cameramen. That's how they gained experience; that's how they made contacts; that's how they established a reputation and became known within the medium. Also, they continue to shoot news stories between documentary assignments.

Yes, some are free-lancers, but they are very, very well established. Quite a few go free-lance after building solid reputations as staff cameramen.

The term "free-lance" reminds us to repeat what may be a familiar warning: if you're burning to be a free-lance documentary moviemaker as well as (or instead of) a cameraman, don't batter your head against the doors of commercial TV. You'll just get it bloody.

Network documentary production, like network news, is a strictly in-house operation. Sure, you've seen the credits of independent documentary producers on network television. You don't need all the fingers of one hand to count 'em, either. They are the very few exceptions that prove the rule (just as on rare occasions some network news operations buy newsfilm from outside sources).

There are other discouraging aspects of these successful independents you should know about. They are not solitary moviemakers like yourselves, but substantial organizations with funds and plant facilities; they have income from other audiovisual operations; and it took them a long time to crack the network ice (which promptly froze over again). Curiously, they are mostly West Coast-based. No, we haven't been able to figure that one out. (Cameramen: this bad news applies to *producers*. The networks do hire free-lance cameramen for documentaries as well as news).

However, there are one or two foot-candles of light at the end of this upward tunnel. Independent stations, even if they're affiliated with a Big 3 network, do not have an inflexible policy of in-house documentary production. The fact is few local stations (except those owned and operated by the networks) have full-time, exclusively documentary staffs. So if you have a good idea for a documentary on a subject of *local* interest; if it is modestly budgeted; if you can sell your ability as well as the subject; then it's possible you'll get a hearing. Yes, those are grudging words of encouragement, but they're all the traffic will bear!

There are alternatives to hacking that long, difficult and by no means sure trail to documentary work in television. You can go after industrial film houses or the other organizations we've mentioned. This approach is not an easy saunter down the garden path either. Conditions change and not always for the better.

Government agencies that used to contract outside A/V work on a one-to-one basis have switched to computerized lists of so-called qualified producers. Several names from these lists are invited to bid, with the contract going to the lowest bidder. One thing this system does is to make it impossible for anyone without a considerable track record to compete. You may well say "ugh!".

The other alternative for pursuing that documentary goal is getting a grant from public television or an arts or cultural foundation. This is still a possibility despite tightening budgets. These organizations have a kindlier attitude toward talented beginners, or may even be mandated to help them, but it's hard to say to what extent this attitude is translated into dollars and cents.

At best, such a grant is very rough going. For one thing, you are competing against many others for that grant dollar.

Then there's the chore of putting your request in writing, the art of "grantsmanship." Before making an application, find out what the rules and regulations are and follow them meticulously. Your application must pass inspection by a fussy bureaucracy in which nitpicking is not unknown.

And *then,* you'll have to wait and wait as your papers pass sluggishly through coils and coils of red tape whose most maddening feature is the endless reviews. These reviews can be compared to a set of Chinese boxes. Open one and there's another; open that one, there's still another. . . and another. . . . It's a good idea to develop an Oriental sense of calm to help you sweat through the long wait.

Oh! Let's not forget you must show evidence of professional skill as part of your application. You're probably better off submitting a documentary you've shot rather than a sample reel. Don't make it too long! Keep it to a half hour or less. It's amazing how much you can tell on film or tape in 20 minutes, or 15, or even 10, if you've planned it all carefully.

There is another way of breaking into documentaries if you don't insist on being your own moviemaker first right off the bat. That is to attach yourself to an established documentarian or to a moviemaker who's been successful in getting assignments and/or grants. You may have to start very humbly—not even as a production assistant but as a "gofer," although both functions are frequently combined; but you've opened the door. You're right—it's another version of the entry level job.

If he's a good moviemaker, you can learn from him; if he's not, stay away since he's bound to be a harmful influence. And if you can't tell the difference, you have no business in this business.

Please don't kid yourself, or let him kid you, that his ability to get work means that he's a good moviemaker. It means he's a good promoter, a successful entrepreneur, nothing else.

That's not to say you can't be a successful business man *and* a good moviemaker, that being creative as well as business-like are qualities that contradict one another. Nonsense! If you free-lance, you have to be hard-headed about the bottom line and you must be aggressive. Otherwise, you'll never stay ahead of the pack coming up the trail after you!

And while we're on the sordid matter of making money, here's another tip: no matter how lowly the role you assume when you join a moviemaker's staff, get paid for your services. Otherwise, as a certain comedian says, there's no respect, from your employer for you or from you for yourself!

SO YOU WANNA SHOOT FEATURES, HUH?

No, we're not going to make fun of those readers who are impatient at the idea of shooting news or documentaries but want to move directly into working on feature films.

We're not going to attempt to discourage you, either. We have the utmost respect for ambition, determination and persistence. Small miracles do happen. It's just that we can't be of much help; our tips are very meager.

We believe that you're sensible enough to know that you can't shoot for the moon right away, that you don't expect to step in and take over the cinematography—or the production or direction—of a multi-million dollar movie.

If your idea is to get your foot inside the studio door by means of an entry level job, that's good thinking. We're glad to say that in this connection you have a break. A great deal of studio shooting for features is done outside Hollywood. Not only in giant cities like New York with its many studio facilities, but in numerous smaller towns. And of course location shooting in all areas of the country has been a commonplace in the decades following World War II.

Eager to generate revenue that leads to tax dollars, many states as well as cities have set up film commissions to entice feature film production with its huge budgets. So look into this; with a little digging you may get some good tips on whom to contact and where and when.

If you're in doubt about how to go about getting this information, call or write a public official or his office: your local state senator or assemblyman, or city hall, state capital or governor's mansion. Don't be shy about it either. Remember you're a voter and a taxpayer!

A rich source of information is to be found in trade journals like *Variety, Film Daily* and others. If they're not available for newstand purchase in your locality, consider subscribing.

In case your heart is set on shooting and nothing else in feature film production, you might consider a long shot. That's to get yourself attached to an established cinematographer also known as a director of photography (DP). Question is how do you get through to this very busy person, especially when there are others like you trying to get his attention?

Remember that he's a free-lancer, so it's not likely he'll give you a lot of his precious time studying the many work samples sent him. We suggest personal, eye-to-eye contact. No, not by camping outside his door or trying to break into a set (that one works only in the movies!).

The ideal way to carry out this plan, but hardly the most practical one for most of you, would be to enroll at the few first-rate film schools where these eminent directors of photography teach or conduct workshops. Unfortunately, practically all these schools are in Southern California.

In recent years, however, college film departments outside "Lotusland" have set up summer workshops or seminars at which DPs have served as professors. Contact your local college to find out whether any such plans are cooking there.

If enrollment is impractical for you, we suggest attending the lectures these distinguished cameramen give on the college circuit. Ask good questions, make intelligent comments during the question-and-answer period that follows his talk; then try to see him immediately afterward. You'll know quickly enough whether you've sparked an interest in you.

There are also many skilled cinematographers who work chiefly in television—shooting movies for TV, situation comedies, entertainment shows and the like.

Although there are more of them than the Hollywood elite, it may be harder to make contact with them. That's because their careers are in full swing; they are still climbing toward the peaks of prestige, while those who may have already reached the top are more likely to regard young hopefuls with a benevolent eye.

LEARN TO LIGHT!

There is one solid tip we can give you if you want to shoot features. Learn to light! Every well-rounded cameraman knows how to light for clarity and balance, to use lighting to support the story being shot, whatever its nature. However, the cinematographer who shoots features must go farther in using lighting creatively to enhance mood, tempo and a sense of time or place.

It is the ability of film to lend itself to this kind of enhancement—"the film look"—that is responsible for the swing back to it from tape for movies made for TV and for commercials.

Film lighting is a very complicated, subtle, often difficult art. Its importance is such that the cinematographer or "lighting cameraman" (as opposed to the "operating cameraman") is now ranked with the writer, director and editor in the creative contributions they make to the feature film.

"Lighting cameraman" and "operating cameraman" mean exactly what they say. The operating cameraman is a skilled, respected technician and if you can attain that job status in feature film production, you are doing very well.

He has nothing to do with lighting, however, but he is under the supervision and control of the man who does, the "lighting cameraman" or cinematographer who is also in charge of camera movement and composition. This overall authority rates him the title of director of photography.

So if you aspire to the status of a DP, immerse yourself in the craft, science and art of lighting, then allow yourself years of experience before you can justly say that your knowledge and skill have reached their peak.

It is true that on big-budget projects such as movies or lavish commercials where full staffs are the rule, the DP can "ride on the back of" his electrician (or "gaffer" in trade jargon) for lighting expertise. But if he has to do his own lighting, usually the case with a non-union crew, he had better know his stuff!

THE STUDIO (TV) CAMERAMAN

To round off our description of job possibilities, there is the TV studio cameraman. Breaking in, of course, presents the usual obstacles and more, if the studio is unionized. There is another consideration you should be aware of, if you are the kind of reader who aspires to be a creative cameraman, or cameraman/director/producer, or whatever.

The TV studio cameraman is a skilled technician. He must know his camera and its lenses, have the ability to move and pan smoothly and frame well. But he does not do so on his own initiative; it is the control room director who literally calls the shots, manipulating the cameraman at his will. Operating skill is what is expected of the studio cameraman, not creativity.

There is no lighting cameraman in a TV studio. That function is performed by a specialist whose title is lighting director or LD. He knows the light-sensitive characteristics of videotape, but he is not a cameraman and need never have been a cameraman.

There is also a difference in the way a lighting cameraman and an LD light a studio set. The lighting cameraman in film lights for each specific camera setup, for a single camera, so to speak (although in action scenes or other scenes that are difficult to stage, several cameras may shoot simultaneously).

In a TV studio, multiple cameras are usually in use for every kind of subject from a news show to a situation comedy. The control room director cuts constantly and instantly from one camera to another, according to script needs. Obviously, the LD cannot light for each camera angle, so he lights the entire area within the working range of the cameras more or less evenly so that there is adequate exposure throughout. Under these circumstances, he cannot create the subtle gradations in light quality by which the lighting cameraman in film enriches the atmosphere or mood of a particular scene.

The lighting director's calling is a very skilled one, but he rarely has the time or the need, really, for the meticulous craftsmanship of the cinematographer.

Bear in mind that if you make it as a news/documentary cameraman for TV, you will not have the services of an LD. It makes no difference that you may be shooting tape, not film. The LD lights in the studio. In the field, *you* must do the lighting, whether you're shooting film or tape, interiors or exteriors. On occasion—usually a special one—you may have the help of an electrician. The responsibility, however, is yours.

We'll sum it up this way: in news/documentary operations, the lighting cameraman must also be the operating cameraman. This is true as well in many other kinds of non-broadcast shooting. You can count on it if there is no obligation to use a full union crew.

GOOD LUCK!

We have run out of tips. We have tried to be practical and realistic as well as informative. In describing the obstacles and disappointments you will encounter, our purpose was not to discourage you, but to prepare you for those "slings and arrows of outrageous fortune" (Shakespeare again) so that you would be ready to cope with them.

Our stresses on hardships and intense competition for jobs in film and television does not change the fact that there are jobs out there, today.

And the outlook for tomorrow is, to put it cautiously, promising. The rapid growth of cable and satellite TV, the advent of the VCR and similar electronic hardware for increased home entertainment augur a tremendous expansion in programming for information and entertainment.

This expansion will lead to an ongoing need for the production talent and technical skills to create and record this programming software.

This continuous need will also be reflected in the non-broadcast, non-theatrical use of film and tape for informational, instructional, promotional, advertising and other utilitarian purposes.

To be sure, job prospects are affected by the state of the economy. But when the economic sun shines, those job prospects will blossom.

We end on that note of cautious optimism.

Good luck and happy job hunting!

OTHER MORGAN & MORGAN BOOKS OF INTEREST

The Art of Infrared Photography: A Comprehensive Guide to the Use of Black & White Infrared Film
by Joseph Paduano
explains the myths associated with this unusual film and details techniques for producing high-quality negatives and prints.
ISBN 0-87100-238-8   **(paper) $12.95**

Color Primer I & II
by Richard D. Zakia and Hollis N. Todd
the techniques of programmed instruction put to work in an attractive, easy presentation of the basic theory and concepts of color.
ISBN 0-87100-021-0   **(paper) $14.95**

Exposure Manual
by J. F. Dunn and G. L. Wakefield
a standard work on camera-exposure determination in a new and largely reillustrated edition that provides an invaluable guide to every photographer—the keen beginner as well as the advanced professional.
ISBN 0-85242-762-X   **(cloth) $18.95**

Photo-Lab-Index: Lifetime Edition
edited by Liliane De Cock
the most comprehensive, accessible, and understandable encyclopedia of photographic methods, procedures, and material available.
ISBN 0-87100-051-2   **(cloth) $59.95**
                    (supplements) U.S.A.—**$24.95**/year & foreign—**$27.95**/year

Photographic Filters
by Leslie Stroebel
the programmed-instruction method, with its reader questions and answers or tasks, as applied to photographic filters, their principles, and practice.
ISBN 0-87100-028-8   **(paper) $14.95**

The New Zone System Manual
by Minor White, Richard D. Zakia, and Peter Lorenz
an up-to-date revision of Minor White's 1961 classic *Zone System Manual* (also available from Morgan & Morgan, in a facsimile), which enables the photographer to previsualize and preplan his pictures from start to finish thereby eliminating costly guesswork as well as trial-and-error methods.
ISBN 0-87100-195-0   **(paper) $18.95**

Zone Systemizer: A Visual Explanation of the Zone System
by John J. Dowdell III and Richard D. Zakia
ingenious, easy-to-use, calibrated dial that helps photographers compute Zone System exposure and development in visual terms—accompanied by an explanatory workbook.
ISBN 0-87100-040-7   **(dial & book, shrink-wrapped) $18.95**